The Philosophy
of Religion

NINIAN SMART is Professor of Religious Studies at the University of Lancaster, and holds a similar concurrent appointment at the University of California in Santa Barbara. He has taught in the universities of Wales, London and Birmingham, and has held visiting posts at Banaras Hindu University and at Yale, Wisconsin, Princeton and Otago, New Zealand. He has been director of research and development projects in religious education in Britain, and has acted as editorial consultant in the planning of *The Long Search,* the BBC television series on world religions. His publications include *Reasons and Faiths, Philosophers and Religious Truth, Mao, The Religious Experience of Mankind, Background to the Long Search* and *The Science of Religion and the Sociology of Knowledge.* With Donald Horder he edited *New Movements in Religious Education.*

The Philosophy of Religion

Ninian Smart

Oxford University Press
New York

First published in the United States and Canada in 1970
by Random House, New York and Toronto

First published in Great Britain in 1979
by Sheldon Press, Marylebone Road, London NW1 4DU

Reissued in the United States in 1979
by Oxford University Press, New York

Printed in Great Britain by
Billing & Sons Limited, Guildford and London

ISBN 0-19-520138-8 (hardcover)
ISBN 0-19-520139-6 (paperback)

Preface ✍

Philosophy can be like a mirror. It can reveal to us the shapes and connexions of the concepts we use. In using concepts we are, so to say, too close to them to understand them fully. By holding up the mirror of philosophy, we can perceive their nature more clearly. I want, in this book, to hold such a mirror up to religion.

What are the distinctive features of religious ideas? Do they here and there contain contradictions? On what possible basis can they be considered true or false? How do they mesh in, if at all, with the other concepts which we use? Such are the questions which typically fall within the ambit of the philosophy of religion.

It happens, however, that the philosophy of religion is largely a Western creation, and the assumption has often therefore been that the major themes are the concepts of God, freedom, and immortality. This selection of major ideas reveals the fact that Western culture has mainly understood religion in terms of the Judeo-Christian tradition. But religion, of course, has a wider and a deeper spread. It ill befits the philosopher to attend merely to the concepts of his own culture. So in this book I shall not only consider questions arising out of theism as understood in the West, but also questions arising out of Eastern and other religions beyond the contemporary West.

The exploration of concepts has in recent times been much indebted to the methods of linguistic analysis, as it is commonly called

—a method associated with the names of philosophers as diverse as A. J. Ayer, Gilbert Ryle, J. L. Austin, John Wisdom, P. F. Strawson, and, of course, Ludwig Wittgenstein. By consequence, there have appeared, since World War II, a number of books and articles on the analysis of religious language: with one or two exceptions, these writings have taken religious language to mean Christian or at least theistic language. I believe that this artificially restricts the philosophy of religion. What about Buddhism? It is a noble and penetrating way of life, but it is not essentially theistic. It is a religion, but it is not Judeo-Christian.

Though I am sympathetic to linguistic analysis in some sense (J. L. Austin was my supervisor at Oxford, and I owe much to his daunting encouragement), I do not believe that the analysis of religious concepts has so far achieved very much. Too often secret apologetic concerns (whether Christian or agnostic) have crept into analysis. Further, it is a consequence of the demand to see concepts in their linguistic context that they should also be viewed in their living, non-linguistic context. One cannot understand religious language without understanding religious practices. Thus linguistic analysis has to go wider; and it cannot fail to involve itself in questions of the history, sociology, psychology, and comparative study of religion.

Therefore in this book I shall go a bit beyond the typical concerns of current philosophers of religion, in two directions. First, I shall introduce material connected with religion outside the Judeo-Christian tradition. Second, I shall discuss questions arising out of such studies as the sociology of religion. I shall thus attempt to view religious concepts in their diverse, living contexts. I shall attempt to relate such an approach to the writings and thoughts of those who are not primarily philosophers, as well as to those of philosophers. It is a bad thing when philosophy is cut off from those who create its subject-matter. Thus the philosophy of science should be related to what scientists think and do. Likewise the philosophy of religion should be related to what religious people think and do.

A decade or more ago I gave a graduate seminar in the Philosophy Department of the University of Wisconsin. It was an interesting experience, for the students who came were nicely divided into those who professed to understand concepts such as *God* and those who professed not to understand them at all. I came to the conclusion, maybe wrong, that the reason for this division was that some kind of sympathetic initiation is needed before people can grasp the meaning of religious concepts. At any rate, it is important for us to discuss questions about understanding religion, before going on to issues about its truth.

Of course, to understand the meaning of something, such as the word "red," we have to know when the word applies: we have to be able to pick out red things, and so to know when "This is red" and "This is not red" are true. In this respect, understanding the meaning of something cannot be separated strictly from knowing when something is true. Meaning and truth are connected. Still, it is useful to make a rough division between problems about the meaning of religion and problems about truth. So the first part of this book will be devoted to questions about understanding and meaning, the second half to issues about truth.

It will serve as an introduction to problems about understanding religious concepts to examine the possibility of defining religion. For if *philosophy* is a term about which there is much dispute, so equally *religion* seems to have many meanings in the minds of those who employ the expression. Thus our first chapter will be on the concept of religion itself.

Lancaster, 1970

For the new edition I have revised the text to remove a few misprints and infelicities, but I have let the argument stand unaltered. If I were to change anything substantially it would be by addition. There is a sense in which the philosophy of religion as I have here pursued it can be seen as a prolegomenon to a systematic theology. But for this it would be important to discuss more than I have done in the present volume the issues arising around history and in particular the idea of God's acting in history.

Lancaster, 1979   NINIAN SMART

Contents ❧

Chapter One

On Understanding the Concept of Religion

How can we philosophise about religion without knowing what it is? Can we arrive at an understanding of it by means of a definition?

This is scarcely probable—as though we could understand science through a short form of words. Would not one have to know a lot of science before one could claim to understand the meaning of science? Likewise, surely one has to know quite a lot about religions before a formula can be of any help.

Or is the problem perhaps not deeper than this? I have used the phrase "know quite a lot *about*": but is knowledge *about* itself sufficient? Do we not have to have experienced the attitudes of faith? And this surely is not just to know about Christianity or Judaism. I can know lots of things about the history and teachings of Christianity without having experienced Christian faith. I can know about Buddhism without knowing Buddhism. So then it may turn out that any definition of religion needs two legs to stand on. One leg is knowledge about the manifestations of religion; the other is knowledge of religion, as it were, from the inside.

Yet this last requirement might superficially seem to make nonsense of the enterprise both of defining and of philosophising about religion. For first, if I have to have faith before I can understand religion, the whole question of truth is preempted in advance. And second, I cannot be on the inside of several religions. Commitment

here excludes commitment there. How then can one know religion
in general from the inside?

We shall see that there are solutions to these problems, and in any
event the special nature of religious understanding can be illuminated through the search for a definition. But we can at least
already draw one moral from this discussion. It is that the philóso-
phy of religion must not be pursued in the abstract: it has to be tied
back to religion and religions as they manifest themselves; just as the
philosophy of science has to do with real science, not with a sche-
matic construct in the mind of the philosopher. For this reason, the
philosophy of religion must draw its examples from the history and
comparative study of religion.

Let us begin with a succinct statement of the late Joachim Wach,
drawing on the definition of religion given by Rudolf Otto. Wach,
in his *Sociology of Religion* (pp. 14–15), writing of definitions of
religion, avers that ". . . the most workable one still appears to be
short and simple: 'Religion is the experience of the Holy.'"[1] He
goes on: "This concept of religion stresses the objective character of
religious experience in contrast to psychological theories of its purely
subjective (illusionary) nature which are so commonly held among
anthropologists."[2]

There are two important claims being made here. First, it is
claimed that one can best define religion in terms of a kind of
experience. Second, this experience is "objective." Does this latter
point mean that we can only define religion properly if we accept
that it is in some sense true?

To say that the experience is not "illusionary" is presumably to say
that it tells us something about reality. In experiencing the Holy we
are not being hallucinated. If at the heart of religion there lies this
experience, then religion itself cannot be regarded as an illusion. Yet
intuitively we surely feel that this way of characterising religion goes
too far. It is surely possible for a sympathetic agnostic to use the
term "religion," to investigate religion, to reject it no doubt. If so,
then he understands religion without conceding the objective character of the experience of the Holy.

Or does he? Perhaps he may concede the objectivity of religious
experience without subscribing to any of the doctrines and myths

which purport both to express this experience and to describe the nature of reality. For already it is noticeable that we want to make some distinction between religion in general and specific religions. Particular religions are in some sense organic systems—each with its own individuality. If they share some sort of resemblance, then we can speak of them as being different manifestations of religion. It is conceivable that a man might concede the worth and truth of religion in general without subscribing to any particular religion (he might value religious experience, but distrust systems).

But then we would ask: What is it that the "objective" experience of the Holy tells us? Simply that the Holy exists? This would seem to be an extreme and nearly empty version of what we might call "abstractive faith." By this I mean the attitude that there is a heart or core of truth in religions which amounts to less than any one religion actually claims. Or put another way it is the attitude that there is a single end or object of religion which religions in their varying ways both point to and over-describe. One can in this way say for example that all religions have God as their end. Of course, God here has to be described less specifically than He is in say Christianity, for Christ is not so easily to be represented as that Being at which all religions aim: the Muslim does not recognise the divinity of Christ. As we shall see, there are acute difficulties in giving any body to such an abstractive faith. But in the meantime we must make another distinction.

Such abstractive faith must be distinguished from another position not altogether dissimilar in certain respects. When I remarked above that God has to be described less specifically than he is in say Christianity, I might be countered by the answer that, for the Christian, Christ *is* perhaps the end or object of all religions. A Christian might say this if he believes that other religions are more than a mass of fallacies and superstitions. If he diagnoses nobility in the strivings and ideals of non-Christian men, then he may well hold that unknowingly they aim at union with Christ, that they have knowledge of God the true description of whom is discoverable in the Christian tradition. We may call this view "reinterpretative faith"—a faith which interprets other faiths in terms of one's own faith. At a later point it will be necessary to return to consider the

logical and factual difficulties confronting this attitude. Suffice it for
the moment to have distinguished it from what I called "abstractive
faith."

Abstractive faith must in some degree be supported by the facts if
it is to be seriously maintained. Here immediately we run into
difficulties, the more body we give to the core of religion. For
example, if we speak of faith in God as somehow characterising
religions, we are confronted by the example of Buddhism, and in
particular Theravada Buddhism. There is here no belief in God.
The supreme value is nirvana. But nirvana is not described as a
personal Being or Creator or Object of worship. It is rather a state
to be realised. How then can we think of faith in God as the core?

We might exclude Buddhism from consideration. We might not
count it a religion, but rather a philosophy or way of life. There are
those who have taken this line, both Buddhists and non-Buddhists.
For those who think of religion in terms of relationship to God or the
gods, there is a case for denying that Buddhism is a religion, for the
essence of it escapes us if we conceive of it as God- or gods-oriented.
But this short way with the problem is not satisfactory, for a number
of reasons.

First, the heart of Buddhist experience is contemplation. The
contemplative life has analogies to contemplative mysticism in the
Hindu tradition, which in turn has analogies to Sufi and Christian
mysticism. (I say *analogies*, not exact similarities: the higher experiences are described differently, though I believe, for reasons which
cannot be fully set out here, that the experiences themselves are
basically alike.) Since mysticism is generally treated as a religious
phenomenon, and since it undoubtedly occurs in religions about
whose description as religions there can be no cavil, there is a case for
treating Buddhism as a religion. Second, some forms of Mahayana
Buddhism involve a pietism remarkably reminiscent of Christian
reliance on God: by a paradox, part of Buddhism moved in a theistic
direction, where by calling on the name of the Buddha in faith one
might gain paradise. It would be inconvenient and unhappy to treat
part of Buddhism as a religion and another part not, for it would
obscure the essential continuity and unity of even the most diverse
forms of Buddhism. Third, Buddhism contains its rituals, myths,
monasteries, temples: it has, so to say, the paraphernalia of faith,

even though that faith is not typically expressed as faith in a god of any sort.

Abstractive faith in God, then, runs up against the facts. One might in addition cite Jainism and one or two other manifestations of religion where it would be impossible to support the abstractive claim about God. Is there a way out for abstractive faith? There are perhaps two.

One way is to reduce the claim—to talk of something much more imprecise than God: Ultimate Reality or the Holy, for example. The other way is to mix in some reinterpretative faith with the abstractive. Might we not say that though Theravadin Buddhists do not think of nirvana as communion with God, that is what it really is? Though a fuller discussion of the hardships liable to afflict reinterpretative faith must wait till later, it is necessary to give a foretaste of them at this point.

First, reinterpretative faith escapes disproof by the facts (in this case the facts about the Buddhist's view of nirvana and his disbelief in a personal Creator) by claiming that the Buddhist misinterprets or fails adequately to interpret his experience of nirvana. But what are the criteria for determining what counts as an adequate interpretation? Reinterpretative faith—as we have seen—rests on the acceptance of a given faith, a given way of looking at the world. The reinterpreter begins from his faith in God and tries to see Buddhism in this light. But equally we might move in the other direction. I have myself heard and read Buddhist and Hindu reinterpretations of Christian experience. Who is to choose between the rival reinterpretations? That is one difficulty.

Another, perhaps more profound one, is this. In seeking an account of the nature of religion, perhaps in the shape of a definition, we want to be in a position to do at least two things—to understand religion and to have a point of departure for evaluating religious concepts and claims. But to understand religion is surely to understand what religions mean to those who participate in them. This means treating their accounts as in a way privileged. Irrespectively of whether we believe that all things are impermanent in the Buddhist sense or that Christ is the Son of God, we want to know what these assertions mean in the context of Buddhist and Christian living. So we do not want to tie ourselves to an account of religion which does not treat the deliverances of religious folk as in this sense privileged. Further, we cannot have a proper point of departure for the evaluation of religious truth-claims if we build into the definition of religion a truth-claim arising from a particular faith among the faiths. (It is true, and we will have to look into this problem later, that there are those who claim that we can never know the truth of religion except through commitment or faith—so that a "neutralist" and detached evaluation of claims is unrealistic. But even if this position were correct, it would no more warrant a definition of religion which secretly includes theistic assumptions than one which secretly includes non-theistic assumptions.)

In brief, abstractive faith has a rather cruel choice. It can give a relatively rich account of the core of religion, say in terms of faith in God; but it does this at the expense of falling foul of the facts. It can only escape them by becoming a form of reinterpretative faith. But then any definition of religion by reference to the supposed core becomes a loaded definition. On the other hand, abstractive faith can posit a very thin, imprecise core. And does not this give religion too thin a substance? Here we can return to consider the case with which we started: the proposed definition of religion as the experience of the Holy.

As we shall see, the proposed definition does not quite give a thin enough account: the search for a core is liable to end in the sands. But already part of our argument hitherto enables us to dispose of the problem of objectivity mentioned by Joachim Wach. For we have tried to show that it is what religion means to those who participate in it that counts, rather than the truth or otherwise of the descriptions of reality which they give. In other words, we are not committed to the truth of some religion or other before we can hope to understand it. We have to take it seriously, but that is another matter. By the same token, we do not need to accept the validity of the experience of the Holy before we can hope to enter into its meaning. There is no need for abstractive *faith*: and as we shall see, there is no great advantage in plumping for the experience of the Holy as the central core.

But, it may be objected, the attempt to give an account of religion, and of religious experience in particular, independently of the acceptance of its validity, is bound to fail, for the following reason. We cannot understand the experience of the Holy unless we have had it; we cannot have it in a detached frame of mind, preempting ourselves from acceptance of the reality of that which we experience. So in order to understand the experience, we have to accept its validity.

Part of this argument is like what we might say about headaches or the color red. I cannot know what the concept *headache* means without having had a headache. Similarly, I cannot know what *red* means without having an experience of red. The man born blind does not know what *red* really means: the best he can do is to learn about light-waves and the grammar of color words. But this is only a superficial understanding of the concept, and does not get to the heart of understanding. So it is argued (by Rudolf Otto himself, among others) that one cannot understand the experience of the Holy, the numinous experience, without having had it.

I think that so far the argument holds good, though perhaps the way it is stated needs some modification. The boundaries of the numinous experience are not clearly defined, so that it flows over into fear and mundane forms of awe. Let us at least say that without experiencing these states one could have no grasp of what the numinous experience is. It is rather the other part of the argument which we have outlined which needs to be criticised.

Supposing for the moment that I have an experience like that of the overwhelming theophany of Krishna described so powerfully in the Eleventh Book of the *Bhagavad-Gita*. Here if anywhere there is an expression of the numinous experience in its strongest and most shattering form. I have, then, this vision of the Godhead of Krishna. No doubt I would take this experience seriously. Its very vividness and terrifying power would prevent me from distancing myself from it. I would be sucked up into it. But does all this entail that Krishna appeared to me? It is psychologically quite possible that I might a few days later shrug it all off as a bad dream, as a mere psychological occurrence. I could believe—I would have to believe —that I had had the experience; but I could believe that it told me nothing about the nature of reality. And this is not just psychologically possible: it is logically consistent. It might be a foolish conclusion, but it would not be a contradictory one.

Hence even if at the time of such an experience it would be psychologically hard or impossible to disbelieve in the contents of the experience, it does not follow from this that having had such an experience entails the acceptance of its validity as revealing something about the nature of God, reality, or whatever, beyond myself. All that we are entitled to say, therefore, is that we need to have experienced numinous feelings or their close analogues in order to understand what the experience of the Holy is like.

I mention the "close analogues" for reasons which will appear later. For it is not necessary always, to gain understanding of an experience which another has had, to have had precisely the same experience (indeed it is arguable that experiences never precisely correspond, because their individual human contexts make a difference, and these never are the same from one person to another). But it is necessary, no doubt, to have had some analogue of the experience. For example, a disease may give someone intense pain in the thigh: if he says "It's like having bad toothache in the thigh" we at least begin to understand what this pain is like. Similarly, the awe we may feel at seeing a film of an H-bomb explosion may serve as an analogue of Arjuna's experience when he believed himself to be confronted by Krishna in his displayed Godhead.

So then we can admit that some direct acquaintance with a certain kind of experience is necessary for the understanding of what the Holy means, without admitting that we have to accept the objectivity of the Holy in the sense presumably intended by Joachim Wach. It is not that I wish to deny this objectivity; it is only that its acceptance is not a prerequisite of understanding. It is necessary, however, to take the idea of the Holy seriously, even if some may have reservations. We should take the religious object or objects seriously, since to treat them otherwise may lead to distortions in the sociology, psychology and philosophy of religion.

The distortions can arise simply because if the observer of social phenomena considers that belief in an unseen world is simply irrational, he will immediately seek an explanation of the belief, not by reference to reasons, but by reference to social or other causes. This move may not be fruitless; but it can be misguided. For what typically counts as an explanation of human conduct has to do not so much with the norms and beliefs that a person ought to accept, but with those that he actually does accept. If we think these that he actually does accept are silly enough, we are inclined to look deeper than we always should. To take a crude example:

It is customary in the Western world to go to the office in long trousers. Suppose someone however goes to work in a fashionable law firm wearing shorts: we treat this as eccentricity. We look for a special explanation. It could have to do with reasons which we accept. Suppose he says his doctor has told him that the skin trouble on his knees will clear up only if he wears shorts. Then we treat his behavior as explicable. But if he gives no such reason, we delve deeper into his psychology. Perhaps there are causes of his eccentricity of which he is not properly aware. We look for causes where before we might have looked for reasons.

Things get more complex when we contemplate a whole society with (to us) peculiar customs. Suppose a key place in such a society is held by the prophet, who gains legitimation from his experiences of what he takes to be the Holy. It is not enough just to say: The Holy does not exist, or: These are illusions. If we say this, we are then liable to seek not for reasons but causes. We may be right; but we may not. After all, such experiences do occur. They are impressive. There is no reason so far to consider the prophets eccentric, though it is worth finding out whether they have any psychological characteristics differentiating them from other members of the society. It remains, then, an open question as to whether such manifestations of prophetism need causal rather than rational explanation, whereas with regard to eccentricity in a society whose norms we accept it is less of an open question. Prima facie the activity of the non-conformist needs special explanation. Consequently, a blanket suspicion, on intellectual and perhaps parochial grounds, of religious experience may introduce a distortion into the empirical study of religion. We are as yet a long way from having proper criteria for determining our methods of approach.

These remarks imply that we have to take seriously the beliefs, norms and experiences which people themselves in a given society or group take seriously. Hence it is surely necessary to take the experience of the Holy seriously.

But as has been pointed out already it is one thing to take the objectivity of the Holy seriously, another thing to believe in it. We

are not committed in advance, in the study of religion, to acceptance
of its central truths.

So far we have treated the idea of the objectivity of the Holy as
meaning that somehow the experience of the Holy tells us about
reality—reveals something "objective" in reality. It is worth noting
that the slippery term "objective" can bear other meanings (as
indeed its opposite "subjective"). To say that the experience of the
Holy is objective can mean, as has just been said, that there really is
something Holy independent of ourselves which is revealed or manifested through the experience. "Objective" here roughly means
"true"; at any rate an objective experience in this sense can be the
basis of a true assertion about the world.

But there is another sense of the term which simply means that
what is given in experience is given as an object. For example, if I
see a pink rat at the end of my bed, this is objective in the sense that
there is an object of my perception, whether or not it actually exists.
Here am I and there is the pink rat (or there the pink rat seems to
be). In this sense of "objective," we allude to the subject-object
structure of a great deal of our experience (not all of it: a state of
depression is experienced, but not as something other than the
experience of it).

A third sense refers to the status which "objective" statements are
supposed to have. That is, those statements which are established
surely by agreed criteria, as distinguished from those that are matters
of opinion, mere intuition, etc. Thus it is common to think, perhaps
confusedly, of scientific claims as objective, while psychological diagnoses are often thought to be rather subjective. Judgments about
morals and art are "subjective," and assertions about tables and rats
are "objective." In this third contrast, objectivity and subjectivity
have to do not so much with what is being claimed, but with the
degree of confirmation, etc., which the claims supposedly have.

These different senses of "objective" are important, because it is
easy to confuse them. It is especially easy to confuse the first and the
second. Because the Holy reveals itself in experience as "out there"
it does not follow that there is anything "out there," just as one can
see a pink rat "out there" without there being a pink rat "out there"
(objectively, in the first sense). As we shall see, not all religious
experience is objective in the second sense, and this is one reason why

there are limits put upon the attempt to define religion in terms of the experience of the Holy (which is an experience of subject-object structure, i.e. objective in the second sense).

Since Wach drew upon Otto, and since Otto has given the classical description of the experience of the Holy, it is now useful to look in a little more detail at the way in which Otto characterised the numinous experience. It is, according to him, a sense of something which is a *mysterium tremendum et fascinans*. It is a *mysterium*, for it is mysterious, set over against man, or as Otto says, "Wholly Other." It is *tremendum*, for it makes us tremble—it is awe-inspiring, fearful. It is also *fascinans*, fascinating, holding out the promise of bliss and blessedness. This brief characterisation should, of course, be read in the context of the whole range of examples Otto gives in his *The Idea of the Holy*.[3] These examples breathe life into his study and give veracity to his attempt to delineate a central feature (for him, *the* central feature) of religious experience and so of religion.

The vision of Isaiah in the Temple, the dumb-founding occurrence to Paul on the road to Damascus, the call of Muhammad, the theophany in the *Bhagavad-Gita*—these and many other cases testify to the form of religious experience which Otto sums up in the above formula. The characteristics of the experience help to explain a lot of things: the sometimes fearful and even non-ethical behavior of God as described in scriptures, the sense of sin, which reflects in the creature the sense of the holiness and majesty of the Other with whom he is confronted, the uncanny nature of much that surrounds religion, the belief in grace as a blessedness which has its source in the Other, the ineffability of the divine mystery, the role of worship in expressing awe, and so on. It is not therefore surprising that Otto's book should have been hailed as a major achievement in the phenomenological study of religion.

However, it is not evident that Otto's account covers all the major and crucial cases of religious experience. He seems to be less successful in dealing with the contemplative mystic, such as the Buddha and Shankara, than with the prophet and the worshipper. For one thing —and here we come back to the second sense of "objectivity"—Otto makes much of the separation between the Other and the creature, between God and man. In this he is right, for it is indeed character-

istic of numinous, prophetic experiences that there is a sense of the
gulf fixed between the experiencer and the Other, just as in worship,
which expresses awe, there is a sense of the gulf fixed between the
worshipper and the Object of worship—a gulf to be bridged, if at all,
by the gracious condescension of the Other. All this characterises
one aspect of the religious life well. But the Buddha did not—judging from the scriptural reports—feel himself to be confronted by an
Other. For him there was no *tremendum*; he did not bow down in
awe before a Wholly Other. His religion was not primarily one of
worship. In his system of ideas and practices, there is no place for
prayer to God, no need for communion with Him. Rather, and as
we have seen, the center of attention is liberation from the impermanences of the world—a liberation dubbed nirvana. Here there is
no subject-object relation. Nirvana is not something "objective" in
this sense.

It also happens that in the Upanishads and in some other phases of
the Hindu tradition, there is a sense of the identification of the
eternal Self with the ground of being, Brahman. Here again the
subject-object distinction is washed away. It is not a matter of
experiencing a Wholly Other, still less a personal Object of devotion.
(It is true that at a lower level of attainment and truth, according to
Advaita Vedanta, ultimate reality is experienced in this personal
form; but in the identity-situation, one transcends this form of
religion.)

In brief, there is evidence to think that Otto has only diagnosed
one form of religious experience. His account of the numinous is
notably less successful in dealing with the contemplative, mystical
experiences of yogins such as the Buddha. There is no *a priori*
reason to think that there is but one major form of religious experience.

It may be replied that Christian and Muslim mystics, such as St.
John of the Cross and al-Hallaj, speak of union with a personal God.
They do not wash out the subject-object distinction. To this reply, I
answer only that we must recall that theistic contemplatives move
within the ambit of theism, of worship, of the numinous. Why
should they not interpret their interior, formless, dazzling obscurity
by reference to their supreme Object of awe, fascination, and loyalty?
It would however be naïve to forget that in the descriptions of

religious experience concepts are used which have a use already, and already have a numinous ambience. There is no *a priori* reason to suppose, even if there is more than one major form of religious experience, they are mutually repellent. Why should they not interact, and certainly at the level of concepts?

This point can be taken further. Suppose in describing an experience, I refer to the birth of Christ in the soul (an idea found in medieval Christian mysticism). Do you suppose that I derive that expression *totally* from my experience here and now? Do I derive it *entirely* from the dazzling obscurity within me that leads me to speak thus? No: for the very concept of Christ refers back to the Incarnation. The Incarnation is attested through scriptures and the traditions of the Church. I do not make up the concept of Christ on my own; and it is not just a label for a psychological event, or some aspect of a psychological event, occurring within my consciousness in a contemplative state. If Christ is also not just Incarnate, but also my Lord, the object of my devotions and worship, then I am hooking my experience on to my whole life of faith and religion. The description I give goes far beyond the datum in experience. This is natural and proper (we do this all the time with descriptions of experience, even so mundanely as when I look at this here in front of me as a typewriter). In brief, the descriptions used in religion are often in an important way *ramified:* they use concepts which branch out far and wide. Thus we can see an experience in a certain context not just as something giving bliss and insight, but as union with the Godhead, or as the attainment of nirvana, or as the birth of Christ in the soul. We must therefore distinguish, or be prepared to distinguish, between the experience itself, so to say, and the way it is viewed through ramified descriptions. The fact that there are varying ramified accounts of mystical experience, some of which latch on to the numinous, does not invalidate the broad distinction which we are here making, between the numinous and the mystical, between the prophet and the contemplative.

There is in addition a theoretical reason why we ought to look for variegation in types of religious experience, and why it is hardly plausible to think of a single core of religion. Since religions vary in doctrines and myths and beliefs, to a surprising extent, and since they are not by any means universally theistic in character, we have to explain why it is they take these diverse forms. If behind the teachings of the Prophets, of Muhammad, of the Buddha, of Shankara, of Lao-Tse, there lay the same form of experience, why did their messages vary so widely? Why the personal God of Judaism and Islam and Christianity? Why his absence in early Buddhism, his subordination in Advaita Vedanta? It is easier to suppose that there are variations in experience, which in part account for the divergences. Further, it is interesting to note that mysticism was not part of early Judaism or Islam, but came in later; conversely, worship and the cult of the Other is absent in early Buddhism, but later makes its appearance. There are reasons in history as well to reject a monolithic conception of religious experience as being the experience of the Holy in Otto's sense.

In short, the definition proposed is, for all its generality, still rather too narrow. We may at this point begin to doubt in any event whether a definition in terms of religious experience is going to succeed. The doubt arises because there does not seem to be a single major form of religious experience. And also, special experiences, however important, are not the only feature of the religious life. Still, it could be that we wanted to concentrate on religious experiences because they are somehow crucial in the development of religion. In other words, it may be that in looking for a definition we are at the same time looking for a kind of explanation.

Now it is not our immediate concern here (which, after all, is philosophical rather than historical) to give an account of the major factors in the genesis of religions. But it is important to note that the assumption of both Joachim Wach, with whom we started, and some others, is that religious experience is somehow primary, both causally and in another way. It is primary as cause, because—to quote Thomas O'Dea (*The Sociology of Religion*) "Religion is man's response to breaking points at which he experiences ultimate and sacred power." [4] He goes on, partly in explication of the thought of Edward Sapir: "Out of this experience religious organizations, ritual practices, beliefs and values evolve." [5] This is not too distant from the different view of the great sociologist Max Weber that the charismatic person plays a crucial part in the genesis of religious movements—and therefore of other movements in society. For the charismatic person in at least some most important instances is one who has had a call or an enlightenment—like Paul, Muhammad, the Buddha, Wesley, and so on: and such calls and enlightenments are experiences. Experience can generate charisma, a quality by virtue of which a person is "set apart from ordinary men and treated as endowed with supernatural, superhuman or at least specifically exceptional powers or qualities . . ." [6] (Max Weber, *The Theory of Social and Economic Organization*). These powers in short can typically derive from experiences and from the effects of experiences. So then, a major view is that religions evolve out of individual experiences, especially of founders, but also in some degree of disciples.

But experiences can be important in a second way, or so it is held. Thus Joachim Wach regards cults, rituals, doctrines, myths, and so on, as means of *expressing* experience. To say that religious experience is expressed in a certain way is not the same as to say that it is the cause of the expression. The two may in some manner go together. Thus if I smile out of happiness, I have a certain experience, no doubt; and my smile expresses that experience. But the experience is not so much the cause of the (facial) expression as the inner side of what my outer behavior betrays. The causes of my happiness this afternoon are causes both of the inner feeling and of the outer expression.

So we are faced with two theses: one is that religious experience is the cause of religious movements—or at least a highly significant cause (like the cause of an accident: it is not the only causal factor—only the one we find to be most significant). The other thesis is that religious rituals and so on are dependent on religious experience: they constitute the expression of it. The two ideas can be conflated into one. It is easy to think that the expression is *caused* by that which it is designed to express. This conflation, not perhaps absent from the thought of Wach and some other sociologists of religion, gives even added emphasis to the centrality of the role of the experiences which we have been discussing. For this reason, it is easy to think of the definition of religion in terms of the experience of the Holy, etc., as not just a definition, but a mode of explanation: a mode of tracing back diverse religious aspects to a single source. It is not just a way of unifying different historical systems (though it fails in this if attention is only paid to the Holy as

understood by Otto): it is also a way of holding together the
different aspects or dimensions of religion—cult, doctrine, myth,
experience—so that they are all essentially traceable to a single
ultimate, namely (of course) religious experience.

There are two reasons to be sceptical of this emphasis on religious
experience. One is historical, the other perhaps philosophical. Not
all religions have founders. Not all faiths originate in charismatic
breakthroughs. Hinduism merges back into a dim antiquity, and
many are the sources which feed its living streams. Maybe Moses
was the founder of Judaism: but its ongoing has diverse causes. It is
true that we should not underestimate the often crucial part played
by original men, whose experience of the ultimate, etc., can impart
not merely charisma but a new dynamism to the processes of religious history. But we should also note, at the historical level, that
though an individual may transcend the past of his culture, he owes
much to it. The Buddha, for example, was a most original, brilliant
and profound teacher, so far as we can judge from the records. But
he also claimed (by the same and other evidences) to stand in a
certain tradition: he was the Enlightened One of his epoch—whence
came that concept? He promised liberation if those who followed
him trod the Eightfold Path: whence came the idea of liberation?
He claimed to give men a new form of yoga: but whence derived his
general ideas of contemplation? He accepted rebirth: whence came
that idea? He was an original teacher, I repeat: but from the point
of view of the history of religions he was not *totally* original, any
more than was Beethoven in the tradition of music. So in the first
instance, it is not quite realistic to divorce charismatic leadership
from what goes before, or religious experience from its milieu. I am
not here saying that Max Weber does this: I am only pointing to a
limitation on the roles of charisma and experience in the explanation
of how religious movements come about. All this, however, leaves
originality and experience with a crucial role to play. That is not to
be controverted. One only needs to reflect on the place of Paul's
conversion in the fabric of events leading to the religious conquest of
the Roman Empire by the Christian faith.

The second, and perhaps philosophical, reason for being a little
suspicious of the appeal to pure experience in explaining the nature
and constitution of religions is that experience by itself is, so to say,

nothing. That is, experience gains its significance not just from its own qualities, but from the context and shape of the ideas by which we interpret and express it. For instance, in seeing a flower in front of me, I am doing more than having red sensations, etc. In so far as I perceive, or imagine myself to perceive, a flower, I am employing a concept. What is standardly taken as a perceptual experience is in this sense more than the conscious buzz of sensations.

Now I am not denying that it is possible for an animal or a baby, as yet unequipped with concepts, to have sensations. But wherever, rightly or wrongly, an experience is treated as cognitive—as making contact, so to say, with reality—it is to be seen under a conceptual aspect. Now what is clear about the dramatic religious experiences which we have been considering is that they appear in cognitive guise: they present themselves as manifesting some reality—be it God, nirvana, the inner nature of things, Christ. So in order to understand what the experiences mean, they must be viewed in their conceptual contexts.

Indeed, as has been hinted already, we cannot speak about the validity of experiences except in relation to the claims which may be made on their basis, even if the claims are sometimes highly abstractive (e.g. that they reveal the Holy). So in a double way religious experiences are connected with concepts: first, because this is how they present themselves as cognitive; second, because the evaluation of them as valid requires reference to the concepts which express their cognitive aspects.

The connection between experience and concepts helps to explain how it is that religious experience in part expresses itself through ritual, cultic and disciplinary patterns of activity. The awe which is generated in the experience of the Holy is also more formally expressed in worship and other rites. It is too simple to suppose that men, having had an experience of the Holy, then create rituals to reexpress and re-create the awe which they felt. Rather, the very guise under which the experience presents itself owes something to the ritual milieu. For instance, the theophany of Krishna mentioned earlier is the manifestation of Krishna as God. The concept of God itself has to be explained in part by the fact that a God typically is the object of worship and adoration. Further, the mythological symbolism through which the experience is described preexisted: it

belonged to a certain religious tradition within the fabric of Hinduism.

The ritual, cultic aspect of religion, then, furnishes in part the
concepts through which experience is interpreted, and the context
therefore in which religious encounters make sense. If sometimes in
the history of religions, experiences of a dramatic sort have given rise
to breakthroughs and new forms of ritual, etc., this has to be seen as a
kind of dialectic between preexisting institutions and the new forces.
Here there is an analogy to the history of science, where new discoveries and theories do not arise absolutely *de novo* but build on what
they in part destroy—the preexisting conceptual scheme.

Hence it is not altogether realistic to see religious experience as the
main root of religion, nor to regard rituals, etc., simply as a mode of
expressing religious experience. Thus the proposed definition of
religion in relation to the experience of the Holy has two weaknesses.
One is that the idea of the Holy is not wide enough to cover at least
one important class of religious experiences. Another is that the
emphasis on experience conceals the way in which necessarily experience occurs in the context of concepts which in part at least derive
their sense from activities such as worship. Can we adapt our
definition in the light of these remarks?

We could for instance define religion not only as the experience of
the Holy, but as typically containing either numinous or contemplative experience, or both, these being seen as cognitive in the light of
concepts used in the activities of worship or contemplation, or both.
Already religion is seen as complex in a triple way: involving experiences, activities, and concepts. We shall shortly have to examine the
question of what kinds of concepts these are. But in the meantime
we may note that a similar problem of understanding may arise in
relation to religious activities as arose in regard to numinous experience, etc. If to understand the numinous, one must have had a
numinous experience or some close analogue, is it not equally to be
argued that one cannot understand the milieu in which the numinous presents itself without having participated somehow in worship
or its close analogues? And does not this bring us back to an earlier
thesis which we rejected—that to understand one must believe? For
how can one worship without accepting the existence of the Object

of worship? In Christian, theistic terms: how can one worship without acknowledging the authority of God?

It might be answered that there is such a thing as make-believe. Does not the anthropologist live with the group he is studying, and participate in their activities as far as possible? In doing this he surely has to accept for the time being with seriousness the myths and rituals which the group employs. Is he not then making-believe? Might it not by the same token be possible to enter sympathetically (though with ultimate reserve) into the life of the Christian or the Buddhist, even though one were neither Christian nor Buddhist? I think this would be possible. But at least this should be said: that to begin to understand the Christian idea of God, one must have a notion of what worship, praise, prayer, etc., are. It would seem extraordinarily difficult (to say the least) to pick up the meanings of these activities simply by observing the outer behavior and imitating it. For worship is more than the outer behavior of singing a hymn: but involves an intentional directedness towards the Object of worship, a sense of humility, a glimpse of blessedness in the Other. These "subjective" aspects of the activity are learned through practice, but not just the outer practice.

Let us consider a parallel. To learn to ride a bicycle one has to ride a bicycle. Now one can understand what riding a bicycle is simply by looking at other folk doing it. It is true that one would hardly know in proper fullness what it is *like* to ride a bicycle from merely observing (the feel of the breeze on one's face, what balancing a bicycle feels like, what the satisfactions are of whizzing along country lanes and so forth). Now could we understand what worship is without understanding what it is *like*? Is there a parallel here to the bicycle case?

Well, we can make a distinction between properly worshipping and only going through the motions; but it is difficult to see how the distinction can be made in relation to riding a bicycle. If I sit on my bicycle, turn the pedals and whizz along the road, it is not possible to say that I am only going through the motions of riding the bicycle: I'm just doing it. On the other hand, I can sing hymns with a superficial air of piety without actually worshipping. I can be secretly thinking: What a load of rubbish this whole business is!

Suppose I am always doing this, and never sincerely or properly worship. Can I be said to know what it is like to worship? No. But can I be said either to understand what it is to worship? To understand this, I have to know what right intention is in worship, and to know this I have to have a concept of the Object of worship —to have some conception of what the Holy is. I have to understand not merely that worship expresses humility (which I may know about in mundane contexts), but a sense of creatureliness, etc. In brief, to understand right intention in worship I have to know what sentiments are to be expressed therein. In other words, I have to know what worship is *like* (what it feels like) in order to understand what it is. This is why the case is not just like that of the riding of a bicycle, where I can understand what it is without knowing what it is like. It is why also we can make the distinction between really worshipping and only going through the motions.

But it may be objected here that the argument has confused knowing what a thing is and knowing how to do it. I can know what it is to ride a bicycle without being able to do so. Why can we not say that we can know what it is to worship without being able to do it? Admittedly, to be able to worship means that one must know what certain sentiments are, i.e. one must have experienced them for oneself. But can we not know what those sentiments are in some other way? Can the observer of worship not understand what right intention is without having himself experienced the sentiments which enter into its constitution?

The answer to this objection can be had from a further example. Suppose a Martian visits this world, and suppose too that he is so constituted as never to experience pain. (Let us leave aside the problem of how he would be viable as a conscious organism under these circumstances.) He might notice that a human friend clutched his jaw, grimacing. Inspection might show him that here was a diseased tooth. He could learn that under some circumstances, humans will put up with lots of inconvenience and expense to get rid of such a diseased tooth. Up to a point the Martian would have understood his human friend's behavior. But he would not know what the human meant by saying "I must get rid of this damnable pain!" The intention of the man's activities towards the dentist's chair would primarily have to do with getting rid of the pain, not getting rid of the tooth. As a secondary intention, yes, get rid of the tooth, but because the tooth brings pain. In brief, the Martian would only have a partial understanding of the human's behavior because of a defective appreciation of the human's intentions. That defective apprehension stems directly from the Martian's lack of acquaintance with the experience of pain. (This is one reason why we find behaviorism so attractive in relation to animals: we only have a dim awareness of what the inner side of animal behavior could be like. This behaviorism is nearly always modified, though, when we deal with domesticated animals, which begin to take on the guise of friends and get a bit humanised.)

So it is arguable that the observer of worship will have a defective understanding of what worship is (for to know that one has to know what it is like), if he does not have acquaintance with the crucial sentiments entering into it. In so far as some "secular" sentiments are analogues—such as feelings of humility, and awe at thunderstorms—the observer already has a point of departure. For a full understanding he must know at first hand what the specific feel of worship (or even more particularly, say, Christian worship) is like. It does therefore seem that to understand religion one must enter into it, though there are doubtless modes of entering (as with the anthropologist) which do not imply full commitment, etc., for life. That is, there is no need to suppose that only the fully committed can understand, a position which would be embarrassing, for it would lead to the following strange result.

If only full belief and commitment can give understanding, religion seemingly becomes either true or meaningless. Or more properly, a given religion seemingly would either be true or meaningless. And how could one possibly deny that which one did not understand? Actually, the consequence of our hypothesis would be a little less than this. It would be as follows. One could only fulfil the condition for judging whether a religion is true or not if one fully believes it. One could thus never be in a proper position to say that a religion is not true or possibly not true. But then it might not be true after all, even if nobody could ever be in a position to say this. This result is indeed strange, and in any case runs up against some special difficulties.

For instance, what do we say, on this hypothesis, about the person who is committed to a faith and then gives it up? Did he first understand it and then cease to do so? But how could he *forget* the meaning of what he knew? Perhaps we should say that he did not really have faith in the first instance, if he fell away thus. This is superficially not an unreasonable move to make, because undoubtedly there are people of weak faith who fall away under stress and so on. But suppose the man had all the marks of faith and piety? Well, we could ask: What are these? What indeed? Perhaps the man of perfect faith does not and never did exist. But if we are trying to say anything worth while by asserting that only full belief and commitment give understanding, we must have in mind some level of belief and commitment, some identifiable marks of this faith. Let us say: Someone as pious and so on as the Archbishop of Canterbury—that is the level we have in mind. But do we not come across equally pious and committed men who lose their faith? And about them do we say that suddenly they no longer knew the meaning of what they had once professed? This is one major difficulty in the hypothesis. (Though we may note that "meaning" is ambiguous, and there may be a sense in which a faith can become meaningless to a person, even if he continues to understand it. Of this more anon.)

This difficulty suggests a deeper and more important one. So far we have tended to think of understanding as an either/or thing: either you understand something or you do not. But this may well be unrealistic, especially in relation to religion.

Noticeably, ordinary language suggests that understanding is a matter of degree. "He understands Arabic pretty well." "He shows a poor grasp of trigonometry." "He has a rather imperfect understanding of the causes which impel him to act in the way he does." Still, we must be careful, for there are varieties of understanding. There is knowing how to do things, as in trigonometry and speaking French. Since there are a lot of things to do within such fields of expertise, it is easy enough to talk about a lot of understanding or little—depending on how many of the things the person can do. But the case of understanding religion is not so much a matter of knowing how to do things. It is more a matter of gaining insight into something. Still, even here it seems reasonable to think of superficial, deep and other degrees of insight, etc., so that we do not need to accept the all-or-nothing-at-all conception of understanding religion. Moreover, it is common enough to think that there is a development of understanding on the part of those involved in religion, as they grow older and more experienced in life. Once we accept this conclusion, we are almost bound to abandon the hypothesis that full belief and commitment is a condition of understanding a religion (though we might still say that full belief and commitment is a condition of full understanding—but who has either of these things?).

It seems then in demanding that those concerned with the study and philosophy of religion should understand what religion is (or what religions are), we neither have in mind the impossible demand for complete understanding nor so low a level that somehow the meaning of what is being said and done is grossly and woodenly missed. There has to be an entering into the spirit of religious experiences and activities. And this, as we have argued, requires some acquaintance with the sentiments pervading these. There must be a form of initiation, if only in sympathetic imagination, into the rites and feelings and ideas which animate a faith.

It is worth stressing the experiential and practical aspects of religion, as the milieu in which key religious concepts are to be understood, since the tendency among philosophers has been to treat religious statements simply as metaphysical assertions. There has been much discussion on proving and disproving and failing to prove the existence of God or a First Cause; much discussion of the meaningfulness of claims about Creation and survival; a great deal of attention paid to issues of how religious utterances are to be verified. But such an intellectualist approach to religious problems creates a peculiar gap—a gap indeed which is one of the major problems of the philosophy of religion. It is the gap between the manifestation of religion in worship, meditation, rites, good works and whatever on the one hand, and the seemingly factual, though mysteriously metaphysical, claims about the nature of reality on the other. On the one hand, the religious person's relationship with God (his conceived relationship with God) is shaped in the practices of faith. Yet on the other hand, what do these earthly activities have to do with claims that God made the world a finite time ago—a proposition which seems to play in the leagues of metaphysical speculation and

scientific cosmology? Are these leagues not far removed from incense and prayer? Perhaps we are wrong just to treat religious
doctrines as metaphysical. Perhaps an intellectualist approach to
problems of religious truth is in error. This has to be discussed. But
at least we know this already—that the philosophy of religion is
essentially about *religion*, and religion as we find it has to do with
prayers and incense and the numinous and worship and practical
conduct. Religion as we find it is embedded in rites, and yoga, and
meditation, and churches, and temples, and monasteries, and music,
and art. It surely contains typically a doctrinal side to it, but the
significance of that side may be missed if it is simply detached from
the living practices which give it special meaning for those who
participate in them. At any rate, it is a question as to how we should
treat the doctrinal side: a question which becomes more acute and
interesting when we begin from the side of religion as manifested in
practice and experience.

If we have to take account of religious experience and ritual (and
other) practice in defining it, we also have to have regard to the
concepts used. Is there perhaps a way in which the ideas of religion,
or some central idea at least, can bring unity to the definition? For it
may not seem altogether satisfactory to treat religious experience as
belonging to one or another category, with no underlying core to
appeal to. It is true that there is no need to be mesmerised by
essences: there is no call always to seek a unity under the words
which we use. There are diverse games—as diverse as patience and
American football—and we would no doubt be hard put to it to find
a single essence constituting them all. The fact that we use a single
word does not entail that the definition has to be simple. If it has to
be disjunctive—to give alternative conditions for the application of
the word in question—this is no tragedy. Indeed it is a reflection of
the flexible, analogical way in which language works. Without this
openness and capacity to pun, to leap beyond the already established
sense, to move sideways from one concept to another, language
would hardly help us much in our search for understanding the many
diverse and novel phenomena and ideas we need to cope with in
living and in the pursuit of knowledge. So we do not need to be
ashamed of the disjunction: the "numinous and/or mystical" in our

adapted definition. Even so it would be nice if there were some way in which the forms of religious experience and activity can be unified. Perhaps the concepts whereby they are interpreted can help.

Though *God* and *nirvana*, for instance, are very different ideas and though they may correspond to rather different forms of religious experience and activity (one worships God, but not nirvana: nirvana is, among other things, the cessation or the promise of the cessation of rebirth, whereas God can at best *give* the cessation of rebirth—the grammar and milieu of the two key concepts differ so widely!)— even so, despite these divergences, it may be possible that they both can be comprehended under some more general concept, which will restore unity to our proposed definition. Are they not in differing modes both referring to the transcendent? But what then is the transcendent?

What is perhaps meant is that both God and nirvana are thought of as somehow lying beyond this world, in (so to say) another world. There might be advantages in tying the definition of religion into some such conception, since it would then exclude Marxism and Humanism, for example; though these systems have certain analogies to traditional religions, they do criticise religion, they are in an important sense anti-religious. It would thus be easier if we defined religion so as to keep them out and so preserve their right to think of themselves as against religion. If we define religion in terms of belief in another world, this does the trick: for neither Humanism nor Marxism believes in another world.

But then what if from a sociological or psychological point of view these systems play the same role as religions? It may be that the social function of Marxism in China is very similar to the role of Christianity in Spain. It may be that the loyalty demanded of the Party member is analogous to the discipline of the Jesuit. It could be that the symbolism of revolution, the eschatology of Marxism, the hope of a new kingdom on earth, the moral commandments, the picture of nature—that all these are recognizably like features of religious faith, doctrine, practice, and commitment. If so, it would be artificial to exclude Marxism and Humanism as religions. It would admittedly be kind to them, in preserving, as we have said, their right to claim to be anti-religious. But this is a small gain, and one which can in any event be maintained by the small requirement that Marxists and Humanists should agree to think of themselves not as criticising religion but rather as criticising *traditional* religions.

We should then be on our guard against producing a merely artificial definition of the subject-matter. It is perhaps not commonly enough realised that important issues can hang on definitions. If the sociology of religion is about religion, and this is self-evident; and if it concerns religion defined in a rather broad way; then sociological theories of religion have to do as much with Soviet Marxism as with Buddhism. This not merely makes a difference to the scope of investigation: it makes a difference to the range of evidence and possible counter-examples to any given theory. Already in this Chapter I have argued for the inclusion of Theravada Buddhism among religions, and we have seen how this makes a difference to any view of religion which sees its focus primarily in gods or God. Likewise, sociological theories about religion would have to pass the test of Soviet Marxism if we are generous enough to include the latter under the head of religion.

But how to choose? There seems an artificial and conventional element in definition, and yet that is not the way we think about truth. But if theories, supposedly true, have to be tested by examples in the field, and if those examples are picked out by definitions, then a conventional and artificial aspect enters into truth. Of course, in one way we are used to this. Truth has to be expressed in words, and words are products of convention—in part at least. Still, there is a greater arbitrariness about the procedure we are at present considering, which is to define a field by a definition, this then making a difference to what we count as good or bad theories, true or false hypotheses, within the field. The only thing to do, I presume, is to notice similarities where they exist. It is an open question as to whether Soviet Marxism should be assimilated to Christianity in relation to its sociological and other effects.

But it still is reasonable to take seriously the Marxist and Humanist rejection of religion; and this importantly has to do with the rejection of another world. There are of course many other factors in the rejection. But this seems to sum them up.

Yet when we look into what is meant by "transcendent" and "another world," we are immediately confronted by difficulties and ambiguities. The *trans-* of *transcendent* indicates that here we deal with something "beyond." Beyond the world? But then what counts as the world? We should note in any event that transcendence is rather a sophisticated concept, not one which is bandied about by the simpler adherents of a faith, and not one found under that name at least in the ethnic religions which constitute so important a part of the fabric of technologically primitive societies. It is a theological concept, and therefore belongs to the milieu of those religions which have well developed doctrinal systems, such as Christianity (though not Christianity in its earliest days), Buddhism and Hinduism. *Transcendent*, then, is a rather technical term. It is to be expected that what the transcendent transcends is already conceived in a rather sophisticated way.

This point can be brought out very clearly in the case of Buddhism. (Jainism and aspects of the Hindu tradition might serve also.) But before going on to this, we should note that we are here concerned with the world as it is conceived, not with the world as it actually is (whatever that is). For if a person believes in something beyond the world, he believes in that which transcends the world as he conceives it. But here we meet the problem that it is not enough to explain this transcendence in terms of "another world" as we have attempted in a preliminary way to do. For one can believe in another world which so to say comprises part of this world. Let me explain, by reference to Buddhism.

Nirvana is not heaven. When the Westerner dreams of another world he very often dreams of heaven (or purgatory or hell—these are bad dreams). He thinks of another world corresponding to this one. Such dreams are not absent from the Indian tradition. But whereas there is some idea in the Christian faith that heaven is where God is, and so genuinely lies beyond the cosmos, the Buddhist (and certain other Indian conceptions say the same) thinks of heavens as compartments of the cosmos, and likewise the numerous purgatories that also teem in the cosmological imagination of Buddhist mythology. Thus heaven is part of the world. Gods dwell there. But heavenly existence, whether for the gods or for those who are blessed with such refined existence as a result of their virtue and piety upon earth or elsewhere, is impermanent. Belonging to the impermanent world, it shares its impermanence. Nirvana on the other hand is the

Permanent. It lies, so to say, beyond heaven. (One does not need to take these metaphorical directions too literally.) It transcends the impermanent world, whereas the "other world" of heaven does not. This is the sense in which "another world" can be part of this world. To put it more clearly, another world can be part of the cosmos. It is the cosmos, or rather cosmic existence, which nirvana transcends. So it is not enough to say that transcendence amounts to the concept of "another world" taken in its most immediate sense.

At the same time, of course, nirvana manifests itself in this world. The saint who attains it displays in his character and conduct the serenity and insight which have assured him permanent liberation from the impermanences and sufferings of ordinary existence. When he deceases, he will be no more as an individual. The flow of impermanent states will somehow be replaced by a Permanent one. So nirvana, though it transcends the world in one way, also is present in it in another—in the lives of those who grasp it. (Here I expound the Theravadin position—some other things are also said in certain Mahayana schools about nirvana which go beyond what I have here attempted to express.)

This rather sophisticated concept of the cosmos, which includes within it "other worlds," shows us the sense in which we may use "transcendent" in regard to nirvana. Now though it is true that theological expositions of theism—Christian, Muslim, Jewish, Hindu —also make use of a similar idea in relation to God, though departing sometimes from rather different cosmologies, it cannot be said that all religions have this idea of transcendence. Or at least they do not possess it in such an explicit form. The Greek gods, it may be recalled, lived on Olympus. And Olympus, though unseen, high up, absent from the immediate environment of the pious, was yet part somehow of the world. For many of the gods, their location is ambiguous, hovering as it were between this world and some other. Consequently, one would have to have a pretty generous and inclusive sense of "transcendent" before it would be right to define the focus of religious attention in terms of it. (Besides, it may be thought, it is a rather formal, even rather empty concept.)

The Buddhist and theistic examples have perhaps made this plain: that to import a theological term like "transcendent" into the definition of religion implies that theology is a universal characteristic of religion. For it is a theological, doctrinal term. But not all religions have developed theologies. It may be answered that the more important religions do, the ones that aim in some way to be universal. That may be so (though we need to ask what the criteria of *importance* are: it is too easy to bring value-judgments into play which merely reflect religious or other prejudgments of the situation). But even if we concede that typically a well-developed religion (note again the implicit value-judgment) has a notion of the transcendent that can be fairly clearly identified, we should also note that much of religious belief and expression is not doctrinal and ethical but mythic in character. In this, the "higher" doctrinal religions share much with ethnic cults which do not pretend to universality. Both in the "higher" religions and the "primitive" there is a strong mythic, symbolic element. And it is useful to take this aspect of religion into account in trying to characterise religion through a definition. We do not in any event want to confine the definition to doctrinal faiths. We would be doing this by implication if we simply referred to the transcendent as the focus of religious experience, whether numinous or contemplative. Fortunately, though, there is a way in which the mythic concept of the unseen shades into the doctrinal idea of the transcendent. (It should not after all surprise us that there is some kind of affinity between myths and doctrines, since myths form part of the substance of those faiths which have provided themselves with relatively sophisticated intellectual formulations of belief. In short, doctrines are a kind of extension of what is in part given in the mythic.)

I have referred to the mythic concept of the unseen. What is meant is roughly this. In myths and symbolic representations of divine and other forces in the world with which men conceive themselves to have relationships, it is notable that they stand for entities which are both manifest and hidden. A god can reveal himself to me (like Krishna in the theophany), but essentially he remains hidden. In performing a rite or sacrament, we see outward actions and symbols, yet the true force of what is done is concealed, unseen, mysterious. Indra (the atmospheric, warrior deity of the *Rig Veda*), is not identified with the thunderbolts he unleashes or with the great storm-clouds piling whitely and darkly into the firmament above the great Panjab plain, but he manifests himself through these phenomena. Nearly everywhere in the mythic aspects of religion we see this tension between the seen and the unseen.

This idea of the unseen is, of course, different from that to which we grow accustomed in our ordinary traffic with the world about us. I can see that oak-tree, but not all of it. Its other side is hidden, and my eyes do not penetrate to the hidden formations of the center of its trunk, which are only revealed when the woodman lays his axe to it. These mundanely unseen characteristics of the world about us are not what is meant by the mythic idea of the unseen. Even going to the other side of the clouds would not reveal Indra. Even chopping into the tree, breaking open the bread of the sacrament, scrutinising the wine drop by drop, travelling beyond the shining firmament—these probings would not be thought seriously to have a chance of revealing the unseen potencies, powers and graces which infest the world in its mythic aspect. The world of myth is our world, but it is our world seen in depth (some might say in childishness, superstition, magic: maybe in some cases—I do not mean anything by way of a value-judgment in speaking here of depth: I am only trying to bring out the way in which the mythic represents the world both as seen and unseen, both our world and in a way another world).

In addition, the mythic view of things does not confine itself to the deepening of trees and thunderstorms. It does not merely transfigure what we here have mundanely. It also provides symbols and stories to delineate the other side of what is here transfigured. If this world is seen under transformation through symbols which deepen it into the mysterious unseen, the other world is seen under symbolic forms drawn from this world. Gods are like men, wielding axes, given to wrath, blessing like priests, full of benediction and mobility, kingly power. These anthropomorphic aspects of much of the mythic representation of the forces on the other side are, however, modified by the realisation that it is the other side that we have to deal with. The symbols are drawn from here to delineate what is there. As the seen is illuminated by the unseen, so the unseen is illuminated by the seen.

This idea of the unseen, naturally, comes under many forms. But it is useful to use the idea, for it helps to show how the notion of the transcendent emerges, so to say, out of it. There is a continuity between the two ideas which helps to assimilate the reference and references of mythic, non-doctrinal religion with doctrinal religion. The mythic concept of the unseen is, as we have noted, not quite literal. It is not the idea of the middle of the oak-tree which we cannot perceive till the woodman lays his axe to it. So somehow the forces delineated through mythic symbolism are not precisely of this world, and they are not properly contained in it. (It is true that Buddhism has reduced the mythic by treating it as perhaps more literal than it really is: so that the heavenly world of the gods, though unseen, is still very much part of this cosmos—one having to go on a further stage for true liberation.)

The mythic is not confined, as has been said, to the more unsophisticated "primitive" faiths (but here again beware the value-judgment). The story of God's leading Israel out of Egypt, the Covenant with Israel, the mysterious salvation-history culminating (for the Christian) in the life, death, and resurrection of Jesus—these stories are replete with the atmosphere of the mythic. The unseen reveals itself on the stage of human history rather than in the clump of oak-trees on yonder hill or in the storm-clouds or in the sacred shrine; the unseen power reveals itself as a single Lord demanding obedience to him alone. But as yet the scriptures do not give us the doctrinal concept of the transcendent in its sophisticated form. God is in heaven, on Mount Sion, in the Holy City, in the high places, in the Tomb. He is here and there, revealing himself in or through the seen. So the mythic points towards the doctrinal concept of transcendence. The unseen merges into the beyond.

Given these explanations, it is perhaps better to use the phrase "transcendently unseen" to try to indicate the typical reference range of religious myths and concepts. This phrase may perhaps serve to bring unification to the disjunction of the numinous and the mystical experiences and their surrounding activities, for both are viewed as giving men a kind of contact with the beyond that is not just invisible in an ordinary way, but reaches somehow beyond the world, however sophisticatedly that may be described and felt.

Does this differentiate religions from Marxism? There is no need for any axe to grind here, on either side of the blade. But it is of interest to see whether mythic and doctrinal ideas of the unseen enter into Marxism. Only lightly. It is true that such concepts as the dialectic, the class-struggle, contradictions in matter and so forth can give the Marxist a feel for unseen powers which help to determine human history and destiny. It is commonly remarked that Marxism has an analogy to Judeo-Christian faith, though it offers a rather different mode of salvation to that traditionally conceived. It is often also criticised from a modern empiricist point of view for its metaphysical, doctrinal character. But what seems to differentiate it from the religions is that the latter not merely have a mythic-doctrinal concept of the unseen, but typically incorporate aims of entering into some kind of conscious relationship with it; and this is where the notion of religious experience becomes important again. The numinous and the mystical are of no special concern to the Marxist. Moreover, there are few rites in Marxism, and those that exist are more for the strengthening of social loyalty than for the promotion of this relationship with the unseen.

Naturally, institutions and movements can change. There is no reason *a priori* why Marxism should not manifest itself as a religion. We have evidence from past history of the great changes which can come over religious and other movements.

We begin now to have a fuller characterisation of religion. It involves typically such experiences as the numinous and the mystical "apprehensions" of reality; the latter is conceived as stretching beyond the manifest world in an unseen, transcendent direction; the approach to the unseen is made through such activities as worship and contemplative techniques; and the description of the unseen (partly dependent, but only partly dependent on the deliverances of religious experience) is provided by mythic and often also doctrinal statements. All this takes us some way towards developing the definition with which we started. Typically also religions are embodied in social institutions; typically too they embody ethical teachings.

By using the term "typically," I am meaning to allow rather off-beat counter-examples. Though typically religion is a group affair of some sort, I do not deny that an individual can have his own private faith. Moreover, it is not to be thought that all individuals in a religious group will share with equal or great intensity the central values of the faith. There may be Catholics in Pisa who rarely if ever have anything in the way of numinous feelings. There may be others who rarely participate in rituals; there may be Buddhists who do not have their sights distantly focussed on nirvana; there may be Baptists in Manitoba who regard the local congregation merely as a kind of club.

What is important from the standpoint of the philosophy of religion in the above attempt to characterise the nature of religion is that there are problems about the connections of the different aspects of religion mentioned. We have discussed one or two of these in relation to the way in which religious experience and ritual has to be understood. If the concept *God* incorporates the idea of holiness and so by implication the numinous response, this will make a difference to our evaluation of the question of God's existence. As a mere First Cause, God may just play a theoretical role in our attempt to understand the world; but then he might be quite dispensable, for it could be that a First Cause can do no good in explaining anything. But if God is somehow a datum of experience, and perhaps of experience of a rather special sort, we look at the question of his existence in quite another way. Or to put the matter in a cruder way: Why should anyone worship a First Cause?

Again, when we note that an important role is played in much of religion by mythic statements and symbols, we must begin to ask how such "poetry" could be true or false. And if such modes of apprehension are used to clothe the expression of religious experience, how can the latter claim to give a valid insight into reality? And if the heart of religion very often has to do with such activities as worship, how do these link up with ethical demands? For at one level, Christianity (for instance) is often represented as a path of conduct; and yet perhaps its heart lies in something different from the pursuit of good citizenship. And again, how can we make sense of claims about the unseen reaches of the world described in mythic and doctrinal language, and aimed at in so much of ritual and sacramental activity? It can already be seen that a realistic appraisal of the actual nature of religion takes us far beyond questions about the truth or otherwise of certain metaphysical statements about the Creation, impermanence and so forth of the world, and beyond an academic discussion of the existence of some detached entity labelled "God."

But the procedure I have adopted here, in moving towards a characterisation of religion as it is found in human history, could be criticised by avant-garde Christians (and maybe others too). I have in mind those who argue for a "religionless Christianity," in part following the thought of the late Dietrich Bonhoeffer, in part developing ideas discoverable in the theology of Karl Barth. According to this position, modern man has gone beyond older religious conceptions. He can no longer take seriously the idea of a supernatural Being who serves as a *deus ex machina* to explain the miraculous, extraordinary and so on. The time has therefore come when Christianity (or rather the Christian Gospel) has to be presented without its religious trappings. Those who follow this line of thought vary in the radicalness of their recommendations about the scrapping of traditional piety. But they would in some measure be agreed on an interpretation of Jesus' mission, which was to challenge the religion of his day. So then it does little good to discuss Christian truth and the Christian way in terms of outmoded forms of religion—forms also which may be for all we know false and vicious, as well as outmoded. By a paradox the most important questions in theology and so the most important questions in the philosophy of religion are no longer really about religion. What merit then is there in my rather painful attempt to delineate religion as it is actually found in human history?

To this there are two or three points of reply. First, it is characteristic of religious traditions to throw up elements of thought and practice which transcend those traditions. A live faith is critical of its milieu. Further, religious concepts by pointing to the beyond, symbolically, doctrinally and in other ways, are always wanting (if I may put it so) not to be taken quite at their face value. They do not want to be treated like metaphors which everyone takes literally. They do not want to say "heaven" and have everyone talking meteorology. This transcendence of what is handed down finds a contemporary instance in Karl Barth's contrast of the Gospel in Christ with empirical Christianity and in Dietrich Bonhoeffer's critique of religion. Second, the supporters of "religionless Christianity" do not typically thereby reject the sacraments and the observances of the Christian community. They regard themselves essentially as belonging to the Church, however much they may criticise the churches. They are, in brief, essentially religious even in their rejection of "religion." (Bonhoeffer directed his own inner thoughts to God and the grace which gave him strength, as it turned out, to bear a martyrdom. In some ways his faith may have been secret and secular, but it was still directed towards the unseen yet ever-present figure of Christ.) Third, in characterising religion as a whole I am not saying that religion as a whole is true. It ill befits the philosopher to prejudge these matters, either favorably or unfavorably. It in no way is inconsistent with the present approach to the philosophy of religion to think that (say) the Gospel is true in some sense and other manifestations of the Other are false or defective. I am not taking sides here; but only arguing that it is necessary to see religion in its embodiment before discussing the way the embodied concepts may or may not apply to reality, give insight, and so on.

The objection, though not decisive, yet should make us reckon that religion, like science, is revisionary. To describe its present state and concepts is not to preempt the future. And very often, by the very fact that there are degrees of understanding, we need to confess that the knowledge (or supposed knowledge) of the religious Object claimed or expressed by those who know it in experience goes beyond the descriptions they and we give. Looking at the matter from the "other side," we must see that if religion is about God, or nirvana, or forces unseen, it may well and necessarily pass beyond its own concepts. If God is creator of the world, he lies beyond its ideas; if nirvana is beyond the impermanent and beyond the world as we ordinarily know it, then it must transcend the feeble attempts which we make, from this side of the river of existence, to describe it. The Further Shore, perhaps, is ineffable, not properly to be caught and delineated in human vocabulary. These considerations should make us sceptical of a simple acceptance of religion as it is usually manifested. Religion goes, so to say, beyond religion.

Though we have discussed certain aspects of the problems of understanding religion—for example, the question of whether it is necessary to enter into the sentiments of religious experience in order to be able to comprehend the meaning of worship, the emphasis has been on what happens on this side of the stream. We have looked at the matter from a human point of view. We have considered the understanding of religion as one might consider the understanding of the customs of a tribe investigated by the anthropologist. But since the concepts of religion outreach themselves in the direction of the unseen, of the transcendently unseen as we have dubbed it, we ought to look at the problem so far as we can from the perspective of the "other shore."

This is perhaps another way of saying that the problem of religion is in part the problem of the ineffable. For if our religious concepts outreach themselves, they somehow go out to what cannot be said. It is indeed a problem as to how we can say something through what cannot be said. Is it sensible to think that in some mysterious manner we can gain knowledge by means which involve destroying the very language we use? Is it perchance feasible to indicate ultimate Reality without describing it? Is God indescribable? Is the Zen Buddhist right in urging us to destroy the concepts we use, so that we can savor pure experience? Is this non-linguistic, non-conceptual ultimate a possible object of religion and of human experience?

These questions are implicitly raised by the transcendence of religion of itself. Although we have tried to give a preliminary set of answers to the problems surrounding the understanding of religion from this side of the shore, we ought also to direct our gaze to the further bank. It may be that the meaninglessness of which religious assertions are sometimes accused derives from the attempt by religious folk to put into words what cannot properly be expressed. And even if these questions may not really be resolved in the case of religion, surely we feel that there is more to the experience of living, more to the nature of the world into which we are projected, than can be expressed in mundane words. To these problems of understanding we now turn.

Notes

1. Joachim Wach, *Sociology of Religion* (Chicago: University of Chicago Press), p. 14.
2. *Ibid.*, p. 15.
3. Rudolf Otto, *The Idea of the Holy* (Oxford, England: Oxford University Press).

4. Thomas F. O'Dea, *The Sociology of Religion* (Englewood Cliffs, N.J.: Prentice-Hall), p. 27.
5. *Ibid.*
6. Max Weber, *The Theory of Social and Economic Organization* (New York: Free Press), p. 358.

Chapter Two ❧

❧ ❧ ❧ On Understanding the Inexpressible

Perhaps because religious language tries to point to the "other shore" it is often paradoxical and even (some would say) self-contradictory. Some recent writers in the philosophy of religion have adopted different attitudes to this situation. On the one hand, the paradoxicality as a sign of the ultimate inexpressibility of religion can be thought of as very much to the point: it is a means of *showing* that inexpressibility. On the other hand, if what is being said is inherently contradictory, how can one properly speak of believing it? One cannot *believe* that squares are circular: how can one *believe* in the Three-in-One or that the changeless Supreme Being enters incarnately the world of change? (Compare the respective contributions of Thomas McPherson and Bernard Williams to the influential *New Essays in Philosophical Theology*.[1]) In brief, one view commends the paradoxes, the other sees in them the essential untenability of faith.

I have used the terms "paradox" and "contradiction." Much may depend on whether key religious assertions contain merely paradoxes or genuine contradictions. Paradoxical utterances are only *seeming* contradictions: they have the form of contradictions, but not their substance. For example, if I say, "It is not true that boys will be boys," I am seeming to deny what is a tautology ("Boys will be boys.") But of course, though this last saw has the look of a mere tautology, it is meaning to say something about the world. It is meaning to say that boys typically behave in certain no doubt rather reprehensible ways. I may be thinking on the contrary that very frequently boys are angelic in their behavior. But I put my thought in what appears to be the denial of the self-evident—hence we call it a paradox.

When Christians assert that God is Three in One, are they intending to assert such a paradox? Here we might express the matter a little differently: it is not that the intention is to give pith and force to a claim by employing a paradox, but that somehow Christians are forced by the "facts" to say that God is Three in One. They are not going out of their way to assert a seeming contradiction—it is rather that revelation and reflection on that revelation has impelled the Church to recognise the appropriateness of this description of the Supreme Being. For did not God reveal himself to men as the Father, the incarnate Son, and then at Pentecost as the Holy Spirit? The seeming contradiction is not gratuitous, nor did the Church entirely feel that it was a real contradiction, for efforts were made to produce a formula to describe the Trinity creedally which would escape the charge of self-contradiction. (Whether this was a successful attempt, is another matter.) There were other aims as well, of course, for the creeds were hammered out in response to heresies which the Church regarded as dangerous to the proper understanding and practice of the faith.

It is not then always the case that the paradoxicality of religious language is designed to point to the inexpressible. Paradoxes may arise from reflection on revelation, experience, etc. Islam has no Trinity doctrine. The paradoxical identification of the Self with Brahman (the Holy Power pervading and sustaining the world) which we find in the Upanishads is not to be found in Buddhism. If paradoxes were all intended merely to point to the inexpressible, they could be of any sort (like "Ultimate Reality is both a tomato and a banana"). The particular paradoxes we have mentioned rather try to show a unity between different facets of faith and experience. The hope no doubt is that such "unificatory paradoxes" (as we shall call them) are free from real contradiction. For, as we have said, one cannot believe what is self-contradictory.

Or can one? It will be immediately replied first that as a matter of fact people do believe contradictory sets of beliefs and second that there is no harm in this in certain circumstances, e.g., in religious contexts where the very idea of the contradictions is to point people beyond human concepts.

Regarding the first side of the objection, it is sufficient surely to admit that though people do as a matter of fact harbor contradictory beliefs they ought not to, at least unless the second side of the objection has any force. Consider an analytic truth or tautology, such as "A bachelor is unmarried." This just has to be true, because of the way the words are. It is simply part of the meaning of "bachelor" that a bachelor is unmarried. Now consider the denial of this utterance: "It is not the case that a bachelor is unmarried." This just has to be false. It is necessarily false. This is the characteristic of self-contradictory utterances, they just have to be false. But one ought not to believe what is false. (That is part of the rules of the belief-game, so to say.) Or rather, how can one believe what one knows to be false?

Now of course a person can fail to realise that his beliefs are contradictory: he can be only dimly aware of some tension in his set of beliefs. If he believes something which looks to him self-contradictory he will secretly perhaps also believe that it is not a genuine contradiction, to be resolved somehow. It is in such ways that people can in fact believe contradictions, though without being properly aware of what is going on. But it still is correct to say that one should not believe (one can hardly believe) what one recognises as a contradiction. That is, unless there is substance in the idea that, e.g., in religion contradictions play a different role, and are somehow respectable. This brings us to the second side of the objection cited above.

Presumably, the contradictions which, on this hypothesis, necessarily crop up in religious discourse are not simply or even the expression of false beliefs—necessarily false ones, at that. They serve the function not of stating something about the ultimate but of *showing* something. Contradictions can be a way of showing that certain concepts just do not apply. More radically they could be used to show that concepts do not apply to God, nirvana, the Void, Brahman, and other religious ultimates. The point is stated in a somewhat different way in a recent monograph by William H. Austin (*Waves, Particles and Paradoxes*), in expounding a conclusion about theological paradoxes which he does not accept: "The affirmation-negation paradox is of fundamental importance in theology, giving expression to the principle that the religious ultimate is beyond all human concepts, so that what is affirmed of it must also be denied." [2] Similarly, T. R. Miles, developing further a position formulated in his *Religion and the Scientific Outlook*, recently claimed: "My own suggestion would be a more thorough application of the *via negativa* and the way of silence. To say that God is transcendent is to emphasise the non-applicability of any concept whatever . . ." [3] Likewise it is common enough in Mahayana Buddhism to stress the failure of human concepts to describe at all Suchness or the Void (hence the use of these negative-sounding and empty terms to refer to the ultimate). Is it consistent with the latter claim that Zen Buddhism should use contradictory and nonsensical riddles to arouse insight in those who follow the path towards the ultimate. Thus a *koan* cited in E. A. Burtt's *The Teachings of the Compassionate Buddha* goes thus:

> Riko, a high government officer of the T'ang dynasty, asked Nansen: "A long time ago a man kept a goose in a bottle. It grew larger and larger until it could not get out of the bottle any more; he did not want to break the bottle, nor did he wish to hurt the goose; how would you get it out?"
> The Master called out, "O Officer!"
> To this Riko at once responded, "Yes."
> "There, it is out!"
> This was the way Nansen produced the goose out of its imprisonment.[4]

But if the religious ultimate cannot be characterised by human concepts (or presumably by *any* concepts: Martians would no doubt be in the same trouble in trying to describe it), why not simply substitute silence for contradictions? Why is the ludicrous to be used when saying nothing would serve?

But already we must see that the silence is silence of a certain sort, as a result of the very definition of the problem. The hypothesis is that though contradictions in general are to be avoided, they have a role in religious discourse. This implies a distinction between the religious context and "ordinary" contexts. This in turn implies that if a silence were substituted for contradiction in bringing out the ineffability of the religious ultimate, it would be silence in the religious context. It would be of no use keeping one's mouth shut in one's bath, or failing to respond to reasonable questions about railroad timetables. The silence would have to be more like the famous oblique and silent responses of Zen masters. It would have to have something like the flavor conveyed in the *koan* cited above.

But even so the silence could surely be misinterpreted. For example, one can be struck dumb by the glory of what is revealed in religious experience. (There are instances of this kind of silence given in Rudolf Otto's *The Idea of the Holy;* [5] but also it is common enough for the mystic to speak of what he finds in his experience as being beyond words, inexpressible.) This sort of dumbness, silence, is not necessarily to be interpreted as conveying the idea that no concepts whatever apply to the religious ultimate. It can often be more like the inexpressibility expressed (paradoxically) when one says such things as "I cannot properly express my gratitude to you" or "This pain is indescribable." The intensity of the feeling or sensation may be such as to outrun the feeble and conventional superlatives which we ordinarily use. But I would not be claiming here that no concepts *whatever* apply to my gratitude or my pain. For one thing, the concepts *gratitude* and *pain* apply.

This is where we run up most sharply against the paradox of religious silence, if taken in the rigorous way outlined—namely as being a mode of affirming that no concepts whatever apply to the religious ultimate. For what is it that one is being silent *about?* How can I say that God is totally indescribable without indicating somehow what it is that is being said to be indescribable? And do I not do this by using the term *God?* But then *God* is a concept. So I am simultaneously saying that God cannot be described and describing him by means of the word "God." Now perhaps we may just see this as a further instance of the contradictions we are forced to employ in dealing with the transcendent. But this answer to the problem hardly suffices, unless we assign a special role to the contradiction itself. If it is just a contradiction, it is necessarily false. To do something better than this, the contradiction must be seen as pointing to the impossibility of applying concepts to . . . But to what? If I state what it is (however vaguely, e.g., through the idea of the transcendent or the religious ultimate) I am already saying

something, by implication, about it. I am characterising it as transcendent. I am then employing a concept to fix what cannot,
according to the hypothesis, be described by concepts. The contradiction reemerges. It is difficult to see how the hypothesis can be
understood at all.

There are three ways, at least, out of this difficulty. One is to try
to argue that words such as "God," "nirvana," etc., do not strictly
express concepts: they are more like labels or proper names. Another
way is to distinguish between first-order and second-order concepts,
with only the latter applying to the religious ultimate. (This way
will be clarified shortly.) The third way is to hold that the religious
ultimate is indicated not by words and concepts, but by the path or
paths through which it is approached (including perhaps in those
paths the mythic symbolism characteristically employed in them).

, Regarding the first way, it is certainly true that "God" is sometimes used as a name rather than a description. This is more obvious
in regard to the proper names, such as Yahweh and Adonis, that one
encounters in the history of religions. But this way out of the
perplexity needs supplementation, if it is to be of any use. For
consider how I apply a label or proper name in more mundane
contexts. I have a means of identifying someone or something. A
baby, perhaps, is born and I can identify it as a separate individual.
Comes the day of christening, and it is given a name. But this name
would be useless by itself. It serves to pick him out just because there
are other ways of picking him out. It is a substitute for (say)
pointing at him. So if we were to treat "God" simply as a proper
name, and not descriptive at all, there must be some way of identifying him. This, perhaps and most plausibly, would be through the
path leading to him—through the religious milieu of whatever faith I
take to be genuine. "God" would then be the proper name of that
Being encountered in the sacraments, etc. But this would seemingly
be reducing the first way to the third mentioned above (and there is
a residual difficulty: if God can be "picked out" through the path,
then there is a way of describing him—namely as the Being picked
out through such-and-such a path).

The second way makes a distinction between first- and second-order concepts. For instance, "wise" would stand for a first-order
concept and "not to be described by concepts such as wise" would be

a second-order concept. It would thus be possible to say that when God is said to be indescribable there is attributed a second-order, not a first-order concept. Thus the religious ultimate is not characterised in any particular way (by such concepts as we use to describe features of the world and of our experience, etc.), save that unlike what we ordinarily encounter it cannot be characterised in any particular way. Though this superficially is a way out of the apparent contradiction contained in the hypothesis we have been discussing, it in practice must be a blind alley. For if God or the religious ultimate is to mean anything in practice—if it is to be attainable in some way through the paths of religion—it must come into relationship with human beings. This relationship is a conscious one: it is universally held in actual religions that the religious ultimate and the unseen are mediated somehow to human experience. This may be by revelation, incarnation, conversion, contemplative ecstasy, etc. The modes may vary from one faith to another and from one person or group to another. Now if it is, for some at least, possible to experience the religious ultimate, the latter is in practice distinguishable from other objects of experience, etc. This being so it is possible to assign to it some first-level concept, such as "holy." Let us consider this point through a rather extreme example.

It is characteristic of many systems of meditation, especially in the Indian tradition, to try to empty the mind of all usual thoughts and perceptions, etc. A person so to say cuts himself off from the ordinary milieu of seeing things, thinking about next weekend, daydreaming, etc. Suppose, then, he attains a state of consciousness which is void of all mental images and thoughts. In one way we might think of it as indescribable, since the words for usual forms of experience do not apply. Thus, if I am thinking about the Battle of the Beresina, it is possible for someone to ask what my picture of it is like. Is the river Beresina broad and muddy? Is there snow on the ground? Do the French troops wear red uniforms? How long are the bayonets? I do not *have* to have such a complex mental picture in thinking of the Beresina, but I can certainly have such a one. It is possible in principle by using the language of external perception, etc., to describe what my image is like. But if my consciousness is emptied of all such, I seem robbed of the language to describe it. But no: not really, for "empty of all such images" itself describes my consciousness, rather dramatically, for the state of consciousness in question is very different from anything we normally are aware of. (This is why the Upanishads refer to this state as like dreamless sleep —for the latter is something we can know about ordinarily, though how we know about it is an interesting question.) So then, even the blankest mediation of the religious ultimate would be describable by contrast with more usual kinds of experience. "Not to be described by ordinary perceptual expressions, etc.," would in fact function as a first-order description of experience. It follows, therefore, that if we are *practically* interested in the religious ultimate we are debarred from simply taking it as indescribable, from the very fact that it is mediated somehow through the path or paths of true religion.

This is where we come to the third way of escaping from the contradiction of seriously trying to affirm that the religious ultimate is totally indescribable. This is to think of the ultimate not as conveyed by words, but as indicated by and through the path or paths of true religion. ("True religion" here would not mean propositionally true religion, but the way to the religious ultimate.) Although this method of solving the problem breaks down, it has a certain force, for it indicates to us afresh that the words of religion need to be understood in a certain milieu. Religious language is rooted in religious practice and experience, etc. So perhaps the situation is a bit like that when we use indexical words like "this" and "that." When I say, "Look at that," the hearer cannot pick out what is meant just by attending to the words. The sentence is not linguistically complete without the non-linguistic context (such as the direction of my gaze); whereas if I say, "Eggs are yellowish in color," the hearer can understand what I am talking about without attending to the direction of my gaze and the like. (Naturally the contrast here is a bit simplified, since what I am getting at, even in apparently linguistically-complete utterances, may have to be gathered from my facial expression and so on.) So it might be plausible to think of religious activities, and symbols, as functioning rather like complex fingers—pointing towards the religious ultimate. This indeed is the basis of one Eastern simile: doctrines and the rest are like a finger pointing at the moon—he who concentrates on the finger misses seeing the moon. Taking this simile very rigorously, it might then be possible to have a reference for religious language and activity without allowing that that which is referred to is describable.

It would, of course, remain something of a puzzlement that de-scriptive-sounding language (such as "God led the Israelites out of Egypt" and "Jesus is the Son of God" and "Nirvana is the cessation of rebirth") is employed in religious contexts, for it surely would invite misunderstanding if all the time the religious ultimate could only be pointed at, not spoken of. And again, what would be the purpose of pointing if there could be no way of approaching that which is pointed at? It is implicit in the Eastern simile described above that there can be direct experience of the "moon"—of the Void or Suchness. It is implicit in the Christian faith that there can be a relationship with God. It is not that somehow the rites of the Church point hopelessly onwards to something which can never be encountered. This being so (and still looking at the matter from the point of view of practical religion), we revert to the earlier argument: that if the religious ultimate is mediated to some people at least in some mode of experience, then it is in some degree describable. It is not therefore totally outside the range of human concepts.

Hence whatever it is that we might hope to do by the use of apparent or real contradictions to convey the indescribability of the religious ultimate, it is not possible to claim that all proper religious language must be of this paradoxical nature. (This even leaving aside the fact that quite a lot of religious language is not descriptive in form, but is constituted by expressions of praise, contrition, etc.) Thus the religious ultimate does not seem to have that degree of unintelligibility suggested by the quotation from T. R. Miles. But we shall see that there remains some force in what Miles is saying, in line with the strong tradition not only in the Christian tradition of the necessity of a "negative way" of indicating the religious ultimate (subtracting predicates from God, so to say, rather than trying to assert anything positive about him). In the meantime, let us con-sider briefly one cause of contradictory language in the context of religion, which ties in with some of the preceding discussion.

Contemplative religion, as we have seen, tends to employ a form of spiritual training which in part aims at emptying consciousness of the usual sorts of thoughts and images. In some phases of Mahayana Buddhism (and especially in Zen), the attempt is made to destroy all human concepts of ultimate reality—except of course for ordinary practical purposes of living we need conventional language. This elimination of concepts is pursued at the theoretical level by Nagarjuna, for example, by trying to show that the key ideas we use to describe and interpret the world, such as *cause*, contain contradictions. At the practical level, there is the Zen use of contradictory and baffling riddles as part of the training of the monk. In both cases contradictions can serve a religious, contemplative end in helping to banish the discursive thoughts and conventional attitudes to the world. In this pragmatic manner, contradictions can help to point onward to the experience of the religious ultimate. These contradictions differ from the "unificatory paradoxes" referred to earlier: they can perhaps be dubbed "the contradictions of spiritual engineering." Neither sort coincides with the "paradox of the religious ultimate" (to use William Austin's phrase).

We have seen that it is impossible to affirm the total indescribability of the religious ultimate, for at least in principle the latter must manifest itself in a determinate mode of revelation or human experience, etc. Why then does the position indicated by the quotation from Miles retain its force? Perhaps for the following reason: that we conceive the religious ultimate not merely as manifesting itself in some form of experience, etc., but also as necessarily transcending that experience. We may describe it in as much as it presents itself to mankind, but it cannot be reduced to such manifestations. Thus, so to say, on the further side of any manifestation there lies the unmanifested religious ultimate, and it is *this* which is essentially indescribable. To put it somewhat concretely: we may affirm that God led the Israelites out of Egypt, but "behind" this event there lies something ultimately mysterious and inscrutable which we cannot hope to comprehend. Concepts apply to God's manifested activity, on this view, but not to his unmanifested essence. This would be a way of reinterpreting the "way of silence" proposed by Miles, to escape the objections which have so far been made. It is not just that God transcends the world: he transcends himself as known to us. There are a number of motives which make the religious wish to maintain this belief in what we may call the "incomprehensible outreach" of God, his essential nature which escapes the grasp of concepts.

One reason arises from worship. Those who believe in a single supreme Object of worship typically are led to regard him as the acme and infinity of holiness. No praise can thus adequately express his glory. There is then a feeling that definitions of God's nature are an attempt to capture and so to restrict that glory. (This motive links up with the sense of "inexpressible" when I say that my gratitude cannot be adequately expressed—God is unspeakable, ineffable, for no feeble words of adoration can express what my response should be to his supreme holiness, etc.)

Again, the drive in theism is to peel away anthropomorphism as a blasphemous and inadequate way of looking on God. The notion of an incomprehensible outreach beyond the manifestations of God is a perpetual check on treating God as finite and simply superhuman.

Yet if there is an aspect of God which cannot be understood, how can anyone claim to believe in it? Can what is not understood be believed? For example, I cannot be said to believe or disbelieve that the square root of 5 is rosy, for the sentence "The square root of 5 is rosy" is simply unintelligible.

It might be possible to solve the problem by applying the contrast between first-order and second-order assertions. For instance I can know a lot of things about a car-engine, or as we might put it, I can know a large number of truths about a car-engine. These would be first-order truths, such as that when the radiator gets overheated, the engine is likely to seize up. But I can also know that there are many things about the car-engine which I do not know. This is a second-order truth that I here know. Of course I do not know the truth of the particular propositions about the car-engine of which I am ignorant, but I can know *that* there are some such propositions. So likewise, it might be claimed that I can know that there is something incomprehensible about God without knowing what it is that I cannot comprehend. I can in this way perfectly well believe what is in part mysterious. For instance, I can believe that God is Creator of the world without knowing how he creates the world. I can believe that everything which I do understand about God is partial —that there is always an incomprehensible aspect to what is believed and understood about God.

A version of this position has been expressed by I. M. Crombie in a couple of important articles, one of them in Flew and MacIntyre's *New Essays in Philosophical Theology*. Here he writes, ". . . in one important sense, when we speak about God, we do not know what we mean (that is, we do not know what that which we are talking about is like), and we do not need to know, because we accept the images, which we employ, on authority." [6] Behind this quotation there is a general doctrine about language about God which can be summarised as follows.

Statements about God are essentially parables. Parables are not literal descriptions of God, nor are they allegories with a point by point application to God. The words of the parable convey their ordinary meaning, but they are referring to something outside human experience and life. Thus if we consider statements about God, we can divide them crudely into subject and predicate ("God" as subject, "is merciful" as predicate) where the parables so to say represent and fill out the predicate. The function of the word "God" is to show the direction of reference, beyond the world. According to Crombie, the parables are given in revelation, but we can have a kind of natural, unrevealed knowledge of the direction of the reference of religious language by reflecting upon the contingency and finitude of the world, which suggests to us something necessary and infinite beyond the world.

This doctrine about religious language might be criticised from the side of epistemology—how we can be said to *know* that the parables apply to God? Is the appeal to the authority of Christ as parable-giver sufficient? Does the supposed contingency of the world show us anything about a transcendent Being? But these questions are more to do with the criteria of religious truth rather than with the nature of religious meaning. The two, as we shall see, cannot be fully divorced, but for the time being let us concentrate on Crombie's thesis as a doctrine about the way in which religious language works. Its present interest for us is primarily that it sets very severe limits on the comprehensibility of assertions about God. We know *that* the parables apply, according to Crombie, but not *how*.

One of his reasons for saying this is that when we normally use language in an extended sense we are able to know something of the new context in which that extended sense occurs: whereas in the case of God we do not know anything of that other context, that "other side." For instance, hot temper is not literally hot. The word "hot" is being given a new sense. But we can understand why, for there is a certain appropriateness in thinking of hot temper as hot rather than cold; and we know the circumstances in which the expression is applied and withheld. We know the difference between what counts as hot temper and what does not. But in the case of God we cannot so to say get behind the parables to have a look to see how it is that they apply. When I use a word in a transferred sense, I must know something about *both* ends of the transfer. But it seems that one end is missing in the case of God.

Now it is fairly clear that the problem arises chiefly from the idea that God is so different from what is ordinarily encountered that he is regarded as radically going beyond the words we use about him. The problem does not arise from the fact that God is different from, say, symphonic music. For although in regard to symphonic music we use words in a transferred or analogical sense—e.g., that a movement is tender—we do not complain that we are ignorant of the other end of the transfer. Why should we complain in the case of God? Is not the numinous experience of the Holy comparable to the experience of music, though different in style and flavor? If we are acquainted with the appropriate religious sentiments, etc., surely we are in a position to use terms such as "Holy," "God" and so on as we encounter the aspect of reality which gives rise to their use. Some people have numinous experiences, just as many folk have musical ones. Why then do we need to worry about the argument that we do not have knowledge of both sides of the transfer when we use words in a transferred sense about the Holy? The problem arises from an *assumption*; and the assumption is that God in himself is incomprehensible, and differs radically in some manner from the parables, images, myths, and experiences or whatever that serve to manifest or delineate him.

Perhaps, though, the assumption has a basis in experience. After all it is common enough for religious people to claim that the manifestations of God themselves reveal that God is mysterious. What is made clear by God about himself is somehow accompanied by heavy suggestions of opaqueness, obscurity, mystery. The essential unknowability of the known here is made known. Let us grant that this is why there is a special problem about God which does not arise when it comes to music and other facets of human experience where we frequently use non-literal language. We are then confronted with the following problem: that the words (such as "loving" and "merciful") which we use about God apply to him somehow, though we do not understand in what way. What we do know is that since God is not like us, his love must be different from human love, and so on.

But then it must not be so different from human love as to evacuate the word "love" of all sense. This is the basis of a celebrated criticism of religious language launched by Antony Flew (*New Essays in Philosophical Theology*), namely that when it comes to the crunch (or rather to a series of crunches) religious assertions die a death by a thousand qualifications.[7] For instance, confronted by the case of a child's needless suffering, the theist is challenged to withdraw his claim that God is loving; but instead of doing this, the theist is liable to take refuge in some sense of "love" which is different from the mundane one—a sense which may allow the compatibility between God's "love" and the suffering of a child (while on the other hand it would be impossible to go on saying that a human father loves his children if he persists in torturing them). In this manner, the claim that God is loving is gradually eroded and dies the death by a thousand qualifications. This, Flew believes, is characteristic of religious language, and arises from the desire to cling to faith even when powerful counter-evidence has been produced. By making faith impervious to falsification in this way the believer evacuates it of real content. This is an instance of the meaninglessness which (it is claimed) attaches to unfalsifiable assertions. A digression on this topic is important, for it will illuminate one strand in philosophical discussions about religion in the last thirty years or so.

The supposed connection between meaning and the capacity of an assertion to be falsified has arisen in modern philosophy not merely from common sense considerations but more importantly from the desire in some quarters to eliminate metaphysics and transcendental claims about "ultimate reality" and so forth. A vivid expression of this desire is to be found in A. J. Ayer's *Language, Truth and Logic*, which argues that only those sentences which can be verified by sense-observation are meaningful (together with tautologies—mathematical truths being considered to be a species of these, their truth arising not from the way the observable world is, but from the meanings of the terms employed).[8] The test of meaning, then, is chiefly verifiability by observation. However, for various reasons, falsification came to be substituted for verification as the main test: for there are many propositions in science of a universal character, such as, "Water freezes at 32° F," which cannot be *conclusively* verified, for one cannot observe all instances of freezing water now and in the future. But one can falsify such a statement, since a contrary instance would disprove the universal proposition. Other considerations too entered into the stress on falsifiability rather than verifiability as the test of meaning. Roughly, the doctrine amounted to this: Only a statement which sticks its neck out and runs the risk of being refuted in sense-experience is meaningful. If a supposed assertion does not do this, then it is a fraud. It is empty, meaningless (unless its truth simply arises from the meanings of the terms used in it). Thus if I say, "There is a fairy at the bottom of my garden," but it turns out that I am thinking of a fairy which cannot be touched, smelled, seen, etc., then no counterevidence could challenge my assertion and so by that very fact it is empty, meaningless.

This, very briefly, is the history behind Flew's attack on religious language as dying typically a death by a thousand qualifications— retreating from counter-evidence and so ending up with pseudo-claims. At any rate, the point can certainly be taken that if a word such as "love" is used in too grossly different a sense of God from that in which it is used of human behavior, etc., it is at best misleading to use the word and at worst an empty fraud.

There is also a good common sense reason to link meaning with truth and falsity, and this serves to make the claim that falsifiability is a criterion of meaningfulness plausible. The reason is that typically in learning the meaning of a word, one has to learn when to use it and when not to use it. One has to learn when it applies and when it does not. As typically language is used to state truths, and not for deception, which in any event is a parasite on truth-telling (if we uttered false propositions all the time there would be no way of deceiving one another, just as we could not counterfeit money that was entirely phoney), the business of learning when to apply a word is also the business of learning when to apply it *correctly, truly*. In this sense, meaning has to do with truth, and by contrast it has to do with falsity. In applying a word to reality I am typically staking a claim, and running the risk of being wrong. So it is fairly natural to link meaningfulness and falsifiability.

But it happens there are severe limitations on the use of falsifiability as the criterion of meaning. First (though this does not immediately concern us here), many meaningful utterances are not candidates for being either true or false. Commands, for instance: if I say, "Shut the door," I am not asserting anything which could either be true or false. Second, we may have to give body to the criterion by specifying what counts as falsification. Generally speaking, those who have used the criterion have been thinking of observation as the means of falsifying utterances. By observation is meant seeing, hearing, etc. (using the senses according to well-established rules of language as to what counts as red, a table, and so on). But the mystic, for example, who claims to have an "interior vision" of ultimate reality is not there doing a bit of observation in that sense. It is thus an open question as to how far the idea of falsification and verification should be restricted; and whether it should be restricted to what is crudely called sense-experience. Third, the idea of falsification may have to be tightened up to mean "conclusive falsification." I can conclusively falsify the claim that all swans are white by observing a black swan. But many assertions which appear to be meaningful are not known to be susceptible of such conclusive falsification. For example, the cosmological theory that the cosmos is "pulsating"—periodically collapsing into a dense mass of matter and then expanding again—cannot be conclusively falsified on the basis of observation; or rather, it could not be if ever it were shown that at some previous time the universe was in this dense condition. The traces of its previously expanded condition would have been destroyed, but it would still be a meaningful hypothesis to think of the cosmos as thus pulsating.

In any event, religious claims are often in principle falsifiable. Thus Christian faith would be destroyed if it were shown that Jesus never lived. It might be objected that though parts of religious belief are in this way sticking their necks out, other and crucial parts are not. For instance, to make sense of the belief that Jesus is God one has to believe in God, who (so to say) lies beyond the Jesus manifested to human experience. It is always possible to detach the "this-worldly" claims of religion from the transcendental ones. How could one ever have evidence of a conclusive kind that the world is created by God, etc.?

Though some recent philosophers have raised such points against the meaningfulness of religion, they are not altogether very powerful ones, for the use of verifiability and falsifiability as criteria of meaning has not worked out too well in any case, for the reasons mentioned above. What *is* important to recognise about the move of dividing off the transcendental aspects of religion from the empirical, this-worldly ones, is that it leads to paradoxical and difficult results. For instance, suppose we treat a supposed experience of God not as the experience of a transcendent reality but simply as a certain sort of psychological event. This mode of treating the manifestation precludes us from using it as evidence for a transcendent reality. The same mode of treatment can be applied everywhere else: Jesus is not to be viewed possibly as Son of God, but as an historical figure; a miracle is simply an unusual event—and so on. This (seemingly quite legitimate) decision to confine the description of religious events, etc., to the "this-worldly" side means that they cannot be evidence of the "other world." But on the other hand, a description of them in terms of the transcendent decides the issue the other way. This peculiar situation perhaps accounts for the division among philosophers as to the sense of religion. From one point of view, nothing could tell us anything about the transcendent; from the other point of view, lots could. From one point of view the transcendent outreach of religious utterances would constitute a core of assertion which cannot latch on to experience at all; and if experience is at all the measure of meaning, that core becomes meaningless.

This is a problem which is of peculiar force today. For there are many invitations, partly because of the progress of a scientific way of investigating the world, to seek an explanation of any given religious experience or event. Can we not "explain away" visions through appeal to some principle or other in psycho-analysis? Can we not look on healing miracles as psychosomatic cures? The invitations are of the form: treat these matters from a this-worldly, empirical point of view and they will fit into place as part of the fabric of empirical knowledge. There is no need for dragging in the "other world" to explain the events of this. We are invited, so to say, to scrape the manifestations of the transcendent world off from the transcendent.

The latter then lies in empty darkness, bereft of substance and meaning.

We shall have in Chapter 6 to consider problems of religious explanation. But in the meantime, the following points should be kept in mind. First, we are at the moment looking not at the truth of religious claims, but at their *meaning*. From the point of view of meaning it is not possible adequately to represent what is being said in religion without recognising the indissoluble connection between the manifestations of the religious ultimate and its transcendent outreach. Attempts to analyse religious language which dispense with the outreach fail. Thus Paul van Buren, in his *The Secular Meaning of the Gospel,* tries to represent Christian language in such a way that doctrines like that of Creation reduce themselves to expressions of attitude towards the world (because of the Christian doctrine, one has a "world-affirming," positive attitude to our environment).[9] This is not an adequate account of how religious language functions, and amounts rather to a recommendation on how to reshape the Christian faith without its transcendental elements. It boils down to a kind of Christian humanism: quite a respectable position to adopt, but not in accordance with the inner logic of religious utterances. In short it effectively separates religion as such from loyalty to Jesus. But, as I have said, this is radical reform, not analysis of meaning.

Second, it is by no means obvious that the relation between the transcendent and its manifestations is one of explanation. The suggestion of naturalistic reductionism (where we simply seek explanations of religious experience in terms of "this-worldly" natural factors, such as psychological ones, etc.) is that it is in *competition* with what is taken to be the traditional religious view. The suggestion is that the function of terms like "God" is to explain peculiar phenomena and experiences. With the growth of the natural and biological sciences we do not need the divine explanations. If in this way religion and science play in the same explanatory league, religion is bound to lose out, because of the known fruitfulness of scientific methods of investigating the world. But do religion and science thus play in the same league? It is by no means obvious that the primary function of terms such as "God" is to plug up gaps in our ignorance. It is by no means obvious that the relation between the religious ultimate and its manifestations is intended in religious language to be an explanatory one. Consider my saying, "I had a strange experience this morning: perhaps the explanation is that God caused it." This is not a typical way of looking at religious experience. I do not of course deny that on occasion, religion has been brought in as a system of explanations in terms of the supernatural. Religious supernaturalism can perhaps be represented as playing in the same league as science, and losing. But it is more appropriate to look on the relation between the transcendent and its manifestations in another way. For instance, for the Christian Jesus reveals the nature of God. It is not that somehow the existence of God is a *causal* explanation of Jesus' activities.

Third, it is by no means clear that natural explanations of religious events rob the latter of their validity, so to say. It is only when they are of a "debunking" kind that we are inclined to have doubts about validity. For example, it used to be said, quite without substance, by Christian critics of Islam that Muhammad was an epileptic. This evil and ignorant charge seemed to dispose nicely of Muhammad's claims to have had revelations from Allah. The prophetic experiences, of Muhammad turn out, on this account, to be no more than delusions brought on by epileptic fits. Still, suppose the theory were true, it would make us a bit sceptical of Muhammad's claims—more sceptical at least than we would be otherwise (though it is still quite imaginable that one sees things of great worth during epileptic attacks, just as some have argued that there is worth and insight to be found in the experiences induced by LSD, etc.). However, these matters concern truth-claims rather than meaning. Let us merely conclude here by saying that as far as meaning goes, religions typically see certain experiences, events, sacraments, etc., as manifestations of the unseen, and as thus having a transcendent outreach beyond the manifested. It is not possible therefore to convey the meaning of what is being claimed by trying to scrape off the manifest from what lies behind (or rather, what is conceived to lie behind) it.

Let us therefore return to the problem of understanding at the point where we digressed into questions about falsification and naturalistic reduction. The problem confronting us is that if we take it that the religious ultimate is wholly other in character from us (and from features of our world), we have no means of claiming that the words used about it (e.g. "Love") have any sense at all. For if they apply in a totally different way to God, their use is not merely unintelligible, but represents a radical equivocation. Let us illustrate the point by a mundane analogy.

Suppose I say that the mountain over there is timid. Well, listeners might let it pass as a piece of poetry. But, I go on, I really mean that "timid" properly describes the mountain: the only thing is that a mountain is so very different from a human being that a mountain's timidity is quite different in character from a human being's timidity. All right, say the listeners, we suppose that you have some strange belief, that mountains are conscious in some way, so that they have mental dispositions analogous to ours. No, I say, I'm not able to explain in what way the word "timid" applies to the mountain—as I've said mountains are very different from us. We have no conception what it would be like to be a mountain.

It would, I think, be readily agreed that my assertion about the mountain is just not intelligible. I could have made it intelligible by saying that we and the mountain share some relevant structure, such as consciousness. (This is what we do in fairy tales and the like: we ascribe consciousness to kettles and trees.) On the basis of this similarity, one might think there was some analogy between human and mountainish timidity. This in any event is how we go on about animals. For we recognise a shared something between the animals and ourselves: they are conscious, living organisms, as we are. Though we recognise that a dog's experiences will be unlike ours, yet we think that there is an analogy—so that by analogy we predicate "timid" and other such expressions of dogs.

It seems to follow that we cannot say that God is *wholly* other from anything in the world. Then there could be no shared something which would serve as a basis for starting an analogy. Also, it may turn out to be linguistically absurd to use the concept of the "wholly other" seriously. (The phrase is used, of course, extensively in Otto; but it is by no means clear that Otto meant it *au pied de la lettre*.)

To say that A is different from B may mean either that it is a different entity or that it is unlike B in its characteristics (in some of its characteristics). Two Cadillacs roll off the assembly line: they are alike in every respect—they are, as we say, the same model; but they are two different things. This is the first sense of difference. Let us call it "non-identity." Out of the same factory there comes a Cadillac and a Buick. These are not just different things, but they are different in their (or some of their) characteristics. Let us call this "qualitative difference." In saying that God is "wholly other," we are meaning to say, I suspect, that God is qualitatively different from anything in the world. But before turning to this, let us pause a moment at the idea of non-identity as applied to God and entities in the world.

There would be some (e.g. the theologian Paul Tillich, Martin Heidegger, and others) who would object to treating God as an entity. God is not a thing, however exalted, or an individual, however supreme, existing in addition to the things and entities of the world. Heidegger thinks that traditional religion has treated God as an entity—hence his being counted an atheist; Tillich made the same critique of much religion, but he made it from within the Christian faith. For Tillich, the treatment of any entity as God, or God as an entity, is idolatrous. God is not *a* being, but being itself. One can doubtless have some sympathy for this position, though it is obscure: sympathy, because it seems another move in the direction of transcending the given, which is characteristic of self-critical religion.

The trouble, though, is to know what "being" means. We are aware of how we use the verb "to be," when we say such things as "Tomorrow is Friday" and "There is a green hill far, far away." We use the verb sometimes as a copula, to join predicate to subject, sometimes in an existential sense. ("There is a . . ." means "A . . . exists.") But does it make any sense to take the present participle and use it as a label for something? It seems just bad grammar, masquerading as philosophical profundity. Consider what would happen if we treated other little words in our language with the same seriousness. What of "of," and "and," and "if"? Why not talk about "ofness," "andness," "ifity"? Such locutions would be nonsensical.

John Macquarrie, in his *Twentieth Century Religious Thought*, replies to similar criticisms which have been made of Tillich and Heidegger by philosophers of a rather analytic turn of mind:

> When Tillich and Heidegger talk about 'being' and 'nothing' or 'non-being,' these terms are not to be understood in their abstract

logical signification—if they were we would indeed land up in nonsense. The terms are to be understood in relation to the significance which they bear in human existence; in the experiences of anxiety and finitude, which bring the shock of possible non-being; and in the wonder for being which this shock awakens, the wonder that there is something and not just nothing.[10]

It may be noted that Macquarrie gives a rather different account of the meaning of being in his later *Principles of Christian Theology.*[11]

Does this defense of the language of "being" save it? It is in effect giving it content by making it have to do with human feelings, such as anxiety, the shock of contemplating that there is something rather than nothing, etc. This in one way is to the good, for it relates this language to the religious context. As we argued earlier, the concept of the religious ultimate has to be approached through the milieu in which it is given sense, and sentiments such as awe are relevant to understanding it. However, it remains obscure what function the particular concept of being serves, beyond underlining the following points (which can in any event be stated without introducing doubtful grammar). First, the religious ultimate transcends the world, and is thus not something discoverable in space and time (whereas our ordinary idea of a thing or person is of something that has spatial and temporal characteristics). Second, theism should criticise its own tendencies to anthropomorphism, and these are encouraged by thinking of God as a person, as though the population of the cosmos were one greater than we had imagined. Third, theism conceives of God as in some way infinite. The suggestion of words like "a being" is that a being is finite. It should incidentally be noted that the language of being does not fit nirvana, and especially nirvana as conceived in the Theravadin tradition. There is no call therefore to think of this language as singularly appropriate to the religious ultimate, wherever that is found. It is in this connection important to realise that certain forms of metaphysical vocabulary, however abstract, can take on the flavor of the particular religious tradition out of which they emerge. It is too easy to be taken in by metaphysics, as though it is culturally neutral. In drawing up one's scheme of thought in terms of being, etc., one may simply be preparing the ground for a reaffirmation of the traditional values of a particular culture. (Neo-colonialism is by no means absent from theology!)

For practical purposes, then, we can without too many qualms, speak of God as non-identical with the world and with the persons existing in the world (though Christianity affirms an identity between Jesus and God—a case of a unificatory paradox, in the sense outlined earlier in this Chapter). However, in saying that God is wholly other, we are more likely to be thinking not of the non-identity of God and us, etc., but of the radical difference of his characteristics from those of ourselves and of other entities in the world. How can we interpret this idea of radical qualitative difference?

An initial trouble is that when I say that A is qualitatively different from B I typically have in mind some relevant characteristics. That is difference has to do with particular respects. For instance, when I say that tangerines are different from oranges, I have in mind that the taste is different, the size, perhaps the texture of the skin. I'm not interested in the fact both tangerines and oranges contain juice, pips, etc. So if one says *tout court* "This differs from that," it is relevant for the listener always to enquire, "In what respect or respects?" My assertion can therefore be filled out thus: "This differs from that in respects *a*, *b* and *c*." These respects have to do with properties, such as color, shape, etc. In brief, one cannot say that God is wholly other from (say) us, without inviting the query: "In what respects?" Well, the answer might be: "In all respects"— is this not what "wholly" implies? Does this mean then we have to spell out the assertion thus: that whereas men have hair, God does not; whereas men have legs, God does not; whereas men eat, God does not . . . and so on? The rigid doctrine of the wholly other would seem, then, to mean that no predicate which can truly be predicated of anything in the world can be predicated truly of God. But this would lead to the following paradox.

As we have seen the concept of the religious ultimate in practice is the concept of something which, though it may lie beyond its manifestations, nevertheless manifests itself in the world here and there and somehow. But if the rigid doctrine of the wholly other were correct, no predicate by which we describe a manifestation of the religious ultimate could be truly predicated of the religious ultimate. We could not, for instance, use the term "holy" of God.

By a paradox, there would be no resemblance between God and his manifestations.

Now the paradox does not in one way follow from the doctrine that no predicate can truly be predicated of God which is truly predicated of anything in the world. It does not follow, because this latter thesis is compatible with the doctrine, which we find in St. Thomas Aquinas, that predicates are used *analogically* of God (e.g., "wise" does not mean here quite what it means when applied to a man, but the sense is not wholly different). This doctrine of analogy is built on the basis of a supposed resemblance between creatures and God, in virtue of the fact that God is cause of creatures and effects resemble causes. It is possible then to hold that when predicates are used of God they never mean exactly what they mean when applied to things in the world, without holding that there can be *no* resemblance between things in the world and God. It might then be that there was some analogy between what we have spoken of as the manifestations of the religious ultimate and the religious ultimate itself.

Still, we have seen that to make this idea work at all, it must somehow be possible to talk of a resemblance between what is discoverable in the world and God (etc.). Thus it is not possible to take "wholly other" in its most rigid sense. It would then be another way of saying that the religious ultimate is totally indescribable. This would certainly rob religious language of its ultimate meaning.

It should be noted that St. Thomas Aquinas thought that he could establish on the basis of reasoning that God is First Cause, etc. This enterprise of natural theology could thus furnish the basis for affirming the resemblance between creatures and God on which the theory of analogy depended. But there is no reason in principle why one has to believe in natural theology, and the supposed proofs of the existence of God, before one can make use of the idea of analogical predication in regard to God. The enterprise of natural theology is to do with the ways in which we come to know things about God, and it can be held with perfect consistency, as many Protestant theologians want to do, that our knowledge about God derives from his revelation of himself in history, etc., and not at all through the exercise of natural reason. But it can still be the case that we want to use words analogically, rather than literally, about God; and it only happens that we learn to use those words in a revealed context only, and perhaps in reference to the sacraments also, which are an extension of revelation.

However, an apparent attraction of the idea of natural theology is that it seems to serve as an alternative route to God. It is like "going behind the scenes" to see roughly how it is that the concepts given in parables or however apply. But earlier we had occasion to hint that this idea of going behind may be a gratuitous difficulty. It was argued that Crombie's thesis in part depends upon the assumption that God in his essence differs incomprehensibly and radically from the picture given of him in parables, etc. But only if he is wholly other, in the rigid sense, can we be said to have no understanding of how the parabolic concepts apply to him. Yet we have seen that this is an untenable view. Consequently, why do we not say: we know what God is like from the parables, etc.? Why think you get a better picture of the house through some unknown backdoor when one can walk through the front?

The question uncovers another root of the problem to which we have paid little attention. The assumption of Crombie and Miles is that we have initially at our disposal a stock of ordinary, mundane language, which can be used in parables. The problem is how to transfer this stock of language in a non-literal manner to a realm as yet unknown and undescribed. Rather similarly the assumption of Aquinas is that we begin, so to say, with the things of this world which we can perceive and try to fight our way up to the First God. Then there is the question of how this-worldly language can be used of what is transcendent. Aquinas was adopting the procedures of Aristotle. Crombie, perhaps, is adopting the position which identifies ordinary language with mundane, secular language.

This way of going about talking of God certainly throws into relief what is important: that many of the words used in religion are not used literally. But it is necessary to ask ourselves what our real linguistic starting point is. Let us consider, however, first what the analogical and non-literal is.

If I say, "I see the point of that joke," I am of course not using "see" literally. What we literally mean by "see" is to do with our eyes, and you do not need eyes to see the point of a joke. There is so to say a segment of language, the language of eyes, seeing, perception; and the most common habitat of "see" is in that segment. But then we also use the term in another segment of language (to do with intellectual and analogous problems, like seeing the solution and the point of a joke). We count this as the non-literal sense, because it is not the most common. (Or sometimes we have a historical sense about which meaning came in first, or some idea of one as more "basic": certainly we have no absolutely tidy mode of distinguishing between literal and non-literal uses: thus for all I know the use of "contact" in "to make contact with"—by communication—is more common now than the use of "contact" in the sense of touch, but we are inclined to think of making contact as less literal than coming into contact with.) When a non-literal use is relatively indispensable, we count it as analogical. When it can fairly easily be translated away, we are inclined to look on it as "merely metaphorical." It is also possible for an analogical use to come to be regarded as the literal, when it has established a certain dominance and commonness. Thus "broadcasting" is now scarcely taken as an analogical term. A person who has been brought up in the city might even think of broadcasting grain as an analogical or metaphorical use of the primary term *broadcasting* in the radio-communication sense.

So we cannot divorce the notion of the non-literal from the idea of different segments and contexts of language. But if all ˙religious terms are analogical, then it follows that somehow religion represents a new segment of language which we come to when we have learned the common uses of words in other segments, and where all the words used are drawn from those other segments. But this is patently false. The fabric of human language already includes religious language; just as the fabric of human living already includes religion. And a number of the key words, so far from being used analogically in religion and literally elsewhere, are used literally in religion and analogically elsewhere.

When I say, "God is holy," I am using "God" and "holy" literally, but when I say that Mao Tse-tung is the god of the Chinese, I am using "god" analogically; and when I say that my son is a "holy terror," I am surely not using "holy" literally. There are lots of other examples—*sacrament, sacrifice, prayer, amen, spiritual, divinity, numen, grace, eternal, hallowed,* etc. And not merely do we have a religious vocabulary already functioning, but we also have the life of people and the life of ritual, etc., which give it meaning and context.

So it is a gross simplification to say that all religious language is somehow non-literal. The problem is not necessarily that of beginning with secular language and then trying to extend its uses to an unknown new segment of discourse. Still, it might be replied that there is a difference between the language of religion and language as properly applied to the religious ultimate. It still remains true that the latter has an incomprehensible outreach, going even beyond literal religious terms like "holy."

Yet, all I wish to argue for the moment is that the problem is wrongly posed by thinking of religious language as parabolic on the one hand and as applied to the wholly other, taken rigidly, on the other hand. It is wrongly posed in this way, because it supposes that the onus is always on stretching out from the literal (parables are literally intelligible stories at one level) towards an unknown X. If this is the problem it is indeed insoluble, for there could never be any means of understanding how the parabolic words apply. But if it is asked: "In what way can we conceive of the X as being a known X?" the natural answer is: "Through its religious manifestations." Here there is a scheme (or rather schemes) of language which is not all analogical and metaphorical, and which has its context in such activities as prayer.

It is interesting that the idea of the parable has played such a prominent part in recent philosophical discussions of religion. (It has an important role not only in the writings of Crombie and Miles, but also in Donald Evans' impressive *The Logic of Self-Involvement*.[12]) It is important to see, though, that parables are only one element in religious language. The Creation story in *Genesis* is not presented as a parable, nor is the salvation-history of Israel. These belong more to the mythic style. The Lord's Prayer is not a parable. Not all Jesus' teachings were cast in parabolic form. And this is only to look at one main religious tradition.

Though parables are not myths, they come close to them. It is characteristic of myths to narrate stories of the divine: parables too are stories, and they are about the divine. The difference lies chiefly in the fact that the parable explicitly invites the hearers not to take the surface meaning as its main point. Some remarks of Macquarrie about symbols in religion are here relevant. He writes in *Principles of Christian Theology*:

In myth itself, the symbol and that which is symbolized have not yet been clearly distinguished. As soon as we recognize a symbol *as a symbol*, we have taken a step back from the myth and emerged from a purely mythological way of thinking and talking. Thus although it is often said that myth is indispensable to the expression of religious truth, this statement is not accurate. What is meant is that religious or theological language cannot dispense with symbols, specifically, the symbols drawn from myth . . . But the fact that these symbols are now understood as symbols and that they can be discussed and illumined in an alternative interpretative language indicates that the person who can handle them in this way has transcended a purely mythical apprehension of the symbols.[13]

What Macquarrie here says about symbols perhaps illuminates the difference between the mythic and the parabolic. The parable is already very much at the stage of inviting the hearers to distinguish between the symbol and that which is symbolized. But if we concentrate *exclusively* on parables we are in inherent difficulties, for we can only make the distinction between the symbol and the symbolized *in theory*, and we cannot know *what* it is that is being symbolized (a reason why Crombie needs his sense of contingency to give at least something of a reference for the parables). Hence the source of that hankering for a method of going behind the scenes. But if on the other hand we recognise the context of the parables—for instance, in the case of the New Testament, the religious tradition, Jesus' use of *Abba*, his prayers, his preachings, the transfiguration, etc.—we already know something of what the parables are about. You cannot tell a parable out of context.

It does not seem then, that in the case of religion we are being asked to believe in what is absolutely incomprehensible. The religious ultimate may lie beyond its manifestations and yet remain in some degree describable, from the very fact that what the religious person takes to be a manifestation of the ultimate is of some determinate character, something of which he must ascribe to the ultimate itself. We should note too that paradoxicality arises precisely because analogies are being used, but it does not arise where literal terms are used.

Thus it is correct both to affirm and deny that God is wise (he is not wise in quite the way we are); but it is not correct to affirm that

God is both holy and not holy. Or at least if one were to say the latter it would amount to something like this: "God is holy, but since a lot of people have an inadequate idea of what holiness is, it is also true that God is not holy—not in their sense." But all this does not bring us to the paradox of the religious ultimate, to which we referrred earlier: namely that we have to *deny* that God has any of the predicates we truly ascribe to him, because he far transcends them, each and every one.

I think myself that it is clearer not to affirm this paradox, but to say rather that the descriptions we use of the religious ultimate are inadequate. What the religious person wants to say is something of this sort—that in the very manifestation of the religious ultimate we are able to see that it is mysterious and not fully to be comprehended. (Actually, this is more in line with theistic religion than non-theistic; but much of the discussion has turned on the question of predications about God.) Thus God is not so to say transparent, even when he makes himself known to us. We can thus judge already that what we say is inadequate. But an inadequate description is not necessarily a false one.

We operate most of the time with a two-valued logic of truth and falsity. Is a statement true or false? It has these two possibilities (well, it might be meaningless, but then it would not really be a statement). Sometimes we say a thing is partly true, but the hidden thought behind this is that somehow what is said can be broken down into a number of statements, some of which are true, some of which are not. But adequacy and inadequacy are matters of degree, so there is no neat tie up between the truth of a statement and its adequacy. Consider the following example.

I have just come from the scene of a railroad disaster, and someone asks me what has happened. I say, "Some people got killed." Undoubtedly what I say is true, but it is a rather poor description and may fail to satisfy the questioner. He wants to know how it happened, where, how many got killed, how many injured there are, whether he can be of any help, and so on. True statements can be full, exiguous, wooden, poor, unhelpful, misleading descriptions. So it is perfectly consistent to hold that what we say about God is both true and inadequate. It does not follow from its inadequacy that we need to deny its truth.

But it is clear that adequacy has to do with the context and the purposes of those involved in communication. If I have been to a cricket match and my boy, who is keen on cricket, asks me for a description of the day's play, the adequacy of what I say is related to the desire the boy has to live through the day vicariously, the success I have in making the scene vivid to him, and so on. Roughly, adequacy depends on the purpose of the description, my capacity as a describer, and the inherent ease or difficulty of describing the subject-matter. I can do my best to bring out the style of a particular player, but so much depends on nuances here that even the best narrator would feel frustrated at the end.

We have, then, to consider in relation to describing the religious ultimate what the purpose is, our own capacities, and the inherent problems. We have so far been concentrating on this last.

But sufficient has perhaps been said to make it plausible to think of statements about the religious ultimate as possibly true, though inadequate. There is no *a priori* reason why God should not show himself to be beyond adequate description (much as the nuances of a musical composition can show themselves to defy full description in our language).

We may conclude, then, that there are ways in which one can understand that which is also in part incomprehensible. The paradox of the religious ultimate can be avoided by a notion of inadequacy. Other paradoxes in religion are either unificatory or contradictions designed for spiritual engineering—helping to realise a certain contemplative state, etc. But perhaps one should add to this list those seeming contradictions which arise in theological systems not so much from the above causes as from inherent tensions. Thus the idea of a good and loving God who is all-powerful runs up against the facts of suffering in the world; the idea of an eternal, changeless Being who yet is incarnated and thus in some way changes contains, to say the least, a tension likewise; God is both necessarily good and only contingently so (in Christ). These tensions might be called "substantive tensions." A certain amount of philosophy of religion has been directed to revealing these, and either trying to establish them as real contradictions (hence the theology in question would have to be false) or trying to show that they are not real contradictions or that alternative theologies can express faith equally well (hence the tensions are not damaging ultimately to religious truth-claims). Since the main issue in such discussions has to do with truth rather than meaning, we shall reserve discussion of examples of substantive tensions for the latter part of this book.

So far we have considered problems of intelligibility and meaning from the direction of the living milieu of religion "on this side" and from the direction of the transcendence of the religious ultimate—its incomprehensible outreach "on the other shore." But still not enough has been said about meaning. Perhaps I can explain why in a rather indirect fashion.

Aristotle remarked, about the mysteries (i.e., the ceremonies through which initiates passed in mystery cults, such as that of Eleusis, near Athens), that the devotee went not so much to learn something as to undergo a change, to experience something. He was no doubt thinking that it was misleading to look on religious "revelation" as the imparting of truths: its object is more to transform the recipient of the revelation. Now hitherto we have also in this book stressed the need for a rich context in considering religious propositions. We have drawn attention to the worship, prayer, and so forth which provide an induction into the meaning of religious utterances. But faith seems to imply more than just understanding what is being said; it seems to involve another way in which a religion or outlook is meaningful. For the Christian, for instance, the idea of the eucharistic sacrament can be understood at one level in the milieu of Church life, etc. But at another level, the sacrament is a meaningful experience for those who are truly faithful. In a broader way, life itself can be seen as meaningful or meaningless. Here the notion of meaning is applied to things other than statements. But it is relevant to the latter, for to understand the full religious context which helps to explicate the meaning of religious utterances one has to understand faith and analogous attitudes, which have, as we have seen, to do with the notion of what may be called "living meaningfulness." For the sake of a tag, we can call the more usual sense of meaning (as applied to language) "sentential meaning."

The great interest among theologians at the present time in existentialism is partly because it seems to have something more directly to say about living meaningfulness, while analytic philosophy has on the whole concerned itself with sentential meaning. Thus we saw earlier that John Macquarrie could defend the use of "being" by Tillich and Heidegger on the grounds that it tied up with notions of anxiety and wonder. It had, in short, to do with attitudes and values that surround (or are supposed to surround) basic questions of life and death.

Confusion between sentential meaning and living meaningfulness —a confusion which is natural because of their connection in religious and quasi-religious contexts—is one reason for thinking that those outside faith cannot understand it. What very often happens to the person who loses faith is that the faith no longer has living meaning for him, but this surely does not imply that he has somehow forgotten the sentential meaning. Yet as we shall see, the deprivation of living meaningfulness can look like a failure to understand sentential meaning any more.

I shall approach the problem of living meaningfulness first at a rather general level, in relation to the concept of the meaning of life. But we shall soon get into more particular senses that tie in with specifically religious questions.

Notes

1. Antony Flew and Alasdair MacIntyre (eds.), *New Essays in Philosophical Theology* (New York: Macmillan); pp. 131–134, "Religion as the Inexpressible" by Thomas McPherson and pp. 187–211, "Tertullian's Paradox" by Bernard Williams.
2. William H. Austin, *Waves, Particles and Paradoxes*, p. 49.
3. T. R. Miles, *Religion and the Scientific Outlook* (New York: Humanities, 1959). The quotation is taken from an article, published more recently, that appeared in *Religious Studies*, 1, 2, p. 150.
4. Edwin A. Burtt (ed.), *The Teachings of the Compassionate Buddha* (New York: New American Library), p. 237.
5. Rudolf Otto, *The Idea of the Holy* (Oxford: Oxford University Press).
6. Ian M. Crombie, in Flew and MacIntyre, *op. cit.*, p. 124.

7. See, for example, Antony Flew, in Flew and MacIntyre, *op. cit.*, pp. 96 ff.
8. A. J. Ayer, *Language, Truth, and Logic* (New York: Dover).
9. Paul van Buren, *The Secular Meaning of the Gospel. An Original Inquiry* (New York: Macmillan).
10. John Macquarrie, *Twentieth Century Religious Thought* (New York: Harper & Row, 1963), p. 368.
11. John Macquarrie, *Principles of Christian Theology* (New York: Scribner), pp. 97 ff.
12. Donald Evans, *The Logic of Self-Involvement.*
13. Macquarrie, *Principles of . . .* , *op. cit.*, p. 122.

Chapter Three ᢒᡈ

ᢒᡈ ᢒᡈ ᢒᡈ On Understanding the Meaning of Life

Since meaning in its proper sense applies primarily to linguistic performances, sentences, etc., it is easy to adopt a short way with the rather obscure phrase "the meaning of life." This short way is to regard the locution as incorporating a category mistake. It is like thinking that the square root of 5 might or might not be rosy. Though the notion of a category mistake (expounded classically in recent times by Gilbert Ryle in *The Concept of Mind*[1] and elsewhere) is fuzzy, yet we surely recognise that certain bits of language just do not go with others: radical context-crossing issues in meaninglessness (or at best jokes). Is the idea of the meaning of life any more acceptable than the idea that the chestnut tree over there *refers* to something? Yet the short way with the meaning of life will not do, for a number of reasons.

The chief reason is that there is a well-established connection between linguistic and non-linguistic notions of meaning. To mean is to intend or purpose—to intend to convey something or other, in the case of language; to do something in the non-linguistic range of cases. This, put crudely, is why it is natural to ask such questions as, "What is the meaning of his behavior? He is acting rather suspiciously." We are trying to discern here, from his behavior, what he is up to, what his aims are, etc. So it could be that questions about the meaning of life are questions about its purpose or purposes.

The use of the singular "*the* meaning of life" may beg a question. Why should it be that life has one and only one purpose? And what does this (sententially) mean? It could mean that there is a single objective or pattern of living which all men ought to aim at. It could be that, for instance, loving one's neighbor is the purpose of life, in this sense. But the phrase could also be taken to imply that the universe somehow has a purpose or plan. Discovering that would be discovering the meaning of life. Certainly this is how many religious apologists talk: only if one believes in God can one believe in a purpose in the universe; only if one believes in a purpose in the universe can one believe that life has a meaning. Hence life for the atheist is essentially meaningless, it is argued.

There is, then, an ambiguity about what "life" means (sententially). On the one hand it can mean living, and in particular it can mean individual living. We have here to ask what it means to say that *my* life has a purpose. And we have to consider why it should be that the purpose of my life should be the same as that of the next man. Surely it is an open question as to whether we should all conform to one pattern of purpose. Here too we should note that there is an ambiguity about "same" in "same purpose"—an ambiguity in line with the distinction drawn in the previous Chapter between two meanings of difference, namely non-identity and qualitative difference. Does "same purpose" mean "identical purpose" or does it mean "qualitatively similar purpose." For instance, if three of us are jointly planning the overthrow of the Peruvian government, we are all acting towards an identical purpose. We want, so to say, to engineer one overthrow of the Peruvian government, not three (my overthrow of it, his overthrow of it, and the other fellow's). On the other hand, if the three of us think that the chief end of life is the pursuit of wine, women, and song, we have qualitatively similar purposes. I do not necessarily pursue his woman; I certainly do not drink the wine that has passed his lips (we might, though, drink out of the same bottle or from the same chateau, but of course this would be different parts of the wine out of the same bottle, etc.). Our purposes would have the same form, would conform to the same model. But this would not be a "joint" enterprise. Our aims would be parallel. On the one hand, then, life can refer to living, and we can think of the purpose of living as subsumable under some general aim. This can either be an identical joint purpose, or it can be a similar purpose.

On the other hand, "life" can refer more widely to the way the world is in relation to us and other living beings, perhaps. When I say that life has many lessons to teach us, I do not just mean that *my* experience teaches me things, but that we learn from the constitution of the world and from the way we exist in the world. Roughly, the meaning (in the sense of purpose) of life would in this case have to do with some overall plan controlling the world and our lives in it. To find the meaning of life would be to find this plan and presumably participate in its ongoing—allying oneself with the overall purpose of the plan. This sense of the meaning or purpose of life is most commonly found in theistic religions. (For how can the world have a plan unless there is a planner? Subtract the Creator, and it hardly makes sense to say that the cosmos has a purpose.) However, there is a less personally express analogue to this idea in Taoism: the Tao is the principle governing nature, and the wise man succeeds in participating in that principle, through the non-action (*wu-wei*) which is the paradoxical source of strength of natural processes, etc.

So far then we have distinguished between individual and joint purposes on the one hand and the idea of a cosmic plan on the other. The latter notion suggests that we, in participating in it, make it our joint purpose. (We become co-workers with God, etc.) Indeed, the notion of the meaning of life in the sense of a divine, cosmic plan implies that we ought to fit our activities into a single joint purpose. But there is no *a priori* reason, it would seem, why, on a non-theistic basis, there should not be many different purposes, whether joint or not. It would be these, presumably, that would give "meaning" to life.

But the discussion up to now has been much too wooden. For it is a great oversimplification just to translate "meaning" into "purpose." For one thing, one can have purposes which yet seem to have lost their meaning. In getting on the train to go to the office, I am adopting a means toward an end. The end is working. In this degree I have a purpose in getting on the train. Yet my work may have, as is said, ceased to mean anything much to me any more. For another thing, "purpose" usually suggests further or even ulterior purpose. If I sneeze in my aunt's face on purpose, this implies that my sneeze is a means to some further end—perhaps the insulting of my aunt. But many of the things we do we do for their own sakes. I do not play cricket to achieve some further end, but because I enjoy it. I do not read philosophy in order to improve my mind or something, but because I think that philosophy is important in itself. And so on. To give a pattern to one's living, then, may not mean that every single thing I do conduces to some great end, but that I try to harmonise a whole lot of satisfactions and ends.

Life on this account would not be so much a strategy (like the strategy in war that aims at one end and one end only—the defeat of the enemy), as an arrangement (like a garden, which is not devoted to the mass-production of tulips, but to the compatible and fine disposition of a variety of plants, including some perhaps in the kitchen-garden that find their justification in needs lying outside the garden: just as we serve our neighbors' as well as our own interests). It might be objected that commitment to achieving an arrangement of realised interests in my own life would itself constitute a strategy. *This* would be my overall aim. True. But in practice, folk are very rarely so singly dedicated to winning the best life for themselves: they make things up as they go along. They act in a piecemeal way, hoping to muddle through to a reasonable harmony of satisfactions. And they weave into their lives wider joint enterprises, as at work and play and in family obligations. They go in for the piecemeal realisation of satisfaction and the piecemeal help of others. But some further distinctions have to be made in the taxonomy of purposes, plans, and interests.

In committing myself to a joint enterprise as the dominant strategy of my life, I may be committing myself to a universal goal or a particular one. For instance, in volunteering for the army in war-time, I may just be committing myself (so much so, of course, as to put my life in peril) to the good of the British people. This is a particular goal. Of course, I may also see this in wider terms. I may think democracy is at stake, that democracy is the only life worth living for mankind—so in fighting the enemy I am helping to realise a destiny for the whole of mankind. I am thereby part of a universal enterprise. True, it is not a universal enterprise in the sense that everyone is involved in it. After all, is the enemy not trying to hinder it? But still it tends to a goal which is for the good of mankind as a whole.

It is probably correct to say that the dominant motif in most people's lives is a combination of piecemeal self-interest and piecemeal commitment to particular (rather than universal) enterprises. But certainly there are some for whom a universal purpose or enterprise is dominant. They are liable to sacrifice their lives for some universal goal (world revolution, the victory of the faith, etc.). But, we may ask again, why should there be some one joint goal for mankind? And how does it help to give meaning and significance to life? Is the life of the Chinese revolutionary somehow more meaningful than that of the Tuscan peasant? It is necessary to revert to the point made earlier, that not all that is meaningful in people's lives has to do with purposes. It is better to say that it has to do with values. Consider the following example.

A man says: "Ballet used to mean a lot to me. Not now. It's somehow gone dead on me." "Dead on you?" his friend asks. "How is that?" "I'm not sure," he replies. "But when I was young and living in London I used to go to Covent Garden and Sadler's Wells two or three times a week. I even remember going to some scruffy suburban theatre to see some African ballet (it wasn't African really: they were all West Indians and American Negroes). I can still remember my disappointment at the first night of Helpmann's *Adam Zero*: it was heralded as something big, but it boiled down to a lot of gimmicks that didn't move me at all. And I didn't like the music. Well, that's how I was. But looking back, I think ballet's very superficial and artificial. I think there's a lot of *prancing* in it. You see how it is? The magic just seems to have worn off. It used to be important and entrancing. Now it is neither. That's what I mean by saying it's gone dead on me. It doesn't mean anything to me any more. If I went to see *Adam Zero* again I wouldn't be disappointed, just bored."

The fact that ballet does not mean anything much any more to someone does not of course imply that he finds life meaningless. But it illustrates what may be meant by meaninglessness—the loss or absence of value. It strikes us most forcibly in the case of loss of value: absences we tend not to notice (for instance, though I am an

ardent supporter of cricket, basketball means nothing to me—but I
scarcely notice, for I don't go and don't read about it, and it rarely
passes through my thoughts). One important aspect of meaninglessness is, then, the failure of what has or could be important, moving
and absorbing to us to be so. In brief, it is where what we do or
could value does not have value any more. This is why I said that
meaningfulness has to do with values, rather than simply with purposes.

It is also why a proper delineation of meaningfulness and meaninglessness cannot be undertaken in a short space, for one would have to
have a proper perspective of the fabric of values, their nature and
interconnections in human life, before one could do so. The feelings
and activities of people are not only variegated, because people differ
in their characters and circumstances, but within a life there is a
changing and complex pattern of feelings and activities, of values.
And the interconnections do not only have to do with what lies
inside the individual, so to say: they also arise out of the objective
nature of the things, etc., towards which these feelings and activities
are directed. For example, the love of a man for a woman may lead
him, through the patterns of society, to marry her. In valuing this
state he is typically hitching on to it the possibility of children, who
themselves will open up to him a whole range of delights and
miseries in addition to the felicities and challenge of his married
relationship. Likewise, a fascination with cars may lead me on to
becoming absorbed in the theory of heat engines. The fabric of
values, then, is highly complex, and has its "objective" as well as its
subjective side. It is not my intention here to attempt a proper
delineation of it. But what can be (inadequately) said about the
sense of meaninglessness is this: that it reaches its intense level, one
where a person may be coming near to saying, "Life does not mean
anything to me any more," where either some very central value has
been destroyed, or where the range as a whole has gone dead (this
may, for instance, occur in cases of mental disease, where a pervasive
listlessness afflicts one). A case of the former could be the death of a
wife.

Consider what happens to someone whose values revolve round his
love for his wife. He is, let us say, a retired bank-manager. He has
left his work and his achievements behind him. His life's twilight is

spent in delightful activities together with his dear wife—they go off to play croquet at Budleigh-Salterton in summer every year and meet old friends and have fierce sunlit encounters. They go to the theatre a lot, and love sitting at home afterwards over a whisky and soda discussing the pros and cons of the play. They potter round their garden, quarrelling a bit at each other's capacity to look after plants. She dies. Suddenly all the things he loved to do he no longer loves. His love has gone. The black void means that life is no longer worth living.

Still, it does not take some such personal and immediate shock to induce a sense of meaninglessness. It can also arise from the contemplation of death and the "non-being" referred to in the previous Chapter in connection with Heidegger and Tillich. It is no doubt a platitude that death mocks us. But platitudes, alas, are often true, and the contemplation of death can induce the following considerations. They may be rather commonplace, but important for all that.

In contemplating my own death, I may be pretty cheerful, except that I may fear the process. After all, I may think: "I'm likely to have lived a reasonable span. Life has been good to me. I've done a lot of the things I wanted to do." Things are not so nice if I think it may be death tomorrow. Think of all the jobs I haven't finished (this book, for instance). My wife and family would be bereaved and perhaps poor. I had been looking forward to so many things. All gone. I really haven't done much good in the world: with a bit longer, perhaps I might have done something. Still, I can take some satisfaction from the thought that my values are bound up with ongoing enterprises and lives, and these will survive my death all right. My family will go on living; philosophy will hardly notice my passing; the study of Buddhism will go on making headway, etc., etc. And then perhaps at this point I will suddenly realise how fragile the values are.

For values are very much embedded in society, and society is no more immortal than I am. Consider the enterprise of physics—the whole organization and intercommunication of men who try to understand better the constitution of the world. The results achieved so far look like stepping stones to the future. But there need be no future. The race could be destroyed in a nuclear holocaust tomorrow. It would seem as if physics had ended as a pointless enterprise (except, as a flicker of consolation, we might think of the bits of good it had done in giving men satisfactions). If the individual escapes despair at his own death by contemplating the survival of the enterprises that have helped to give his life meaning, we cannot escape despair at contemplating the destruction of the whole of society. (This incidentally is why old people who have lived through big social changes often feel that their lives are robbed of meaning: the festivals they used to celebrate no longer occur or mean anything to the new generation; how can one explain what a glory and a joy it was to be the May Queen?) There is a kind of vertigo induced in contemplating the cooling of the sun, and the perishing of life on this planet.

Naturally, cheerfulness keeps creeping in. The contemplation of universal death does not have the same emotional impact as the destruction of a loved one, etc. But it gives us at least a glimpse of the decay of all our values, *sub specie mortis*. "Eat, drink, and be merry" affords small consolation, for the prescription thins down ridiculously the scope of our values and purposes.

A similar conclusion can be drawn in regard to disvalues, i.e. to those that we seek to avoid and eliminate. I can make sense of suffering if it is for some end—if my suffering furthers the cause of the revolution, or what have you. But if it is just blind, pointless suffering out of which I can see no good coming, how can I weave it into the fabric of values that gives my life meaning? If, then, our strivings for a better life for mankind are suddenly cut off by universal death, they look to have been meaningless. Perhaps one of the most harrowing communications of this despair is to be found in Nevil Shute's novel *On the Beach*, depicting the slow and painful demise of the remnants of human civilisation after the next war.

The contemplation of universal death is one of the "meditative" ways of glimpsing meaninglessness. There are others which we shall come to. But as we have seen, meaninglessness much more powerfully can afflict a person because of some tragedy or upheaval. Or it can haunt people without their setting themselves to meditate—there are many folk today haunted by the H-bomb, with its implied threat to the whole fabric of their existence.

If death is a boundary situation, there are also boundary or limiting questions which similarly connect up with the sense of meaninglessness. An interesting discussion of such limiting questions is to be found in Stephen Toulmin's *An Examination of the Place of Reason in Ethics*,[2] and some intriguing comments on it are to be found in the first essay of the theologian Schubert M. Ogden's *The Reality of God, and Other Essays*.[3]

According to Toulmin's exegesis of the nature of moral reasoning, one can give reasons as to why an act is right or wrong, and a system of morals can constitute thus a chain of reasons, going up to first moral principles. But as well as the properly moral questions which we can ask, there are the limiting questions which may be asked, as to why I should be moral at all. This is not a kind of question that can be answered within morals, for it is a question which occurs when all the moral answers and explanations have been given. If I ask why I should keep my promise, and someone gives me all the reasons, and I *still* persist in asking, I have as it were reached the boundary of moral discourse. On Toulmin's view, religious assertions have to do with these limiting questions, in morals and elsewhere (for in science too one can reach the boundary and go on asking when all the scientific answers have been given). Thus he writes (*An Examination of the Place of Reason in Ethics*) that ". . . over matters of duty which are not to be justified further in ethical terms, it is for religion to help us to embrace them—and so feel like accepting them." [4] Religion gives a kind of reassurance and confidence, and speaks to the condition of those who in actual living are afflicted by the sense of despair and meaninglessness. The questions, that is, are not just academic. As when a dear one dies, we may ask, "Why did it have to be so?" even when all the answers (it was a virus which attacked the central nervous system, picked up while swimming, etc.) have been given. Still, though the questions are not academic, one can see how they arise by examining the structure of moral and scientific discourse, etc., so that here too there seems to be (if Toulmin is right) the possibility of a meditative way of glimpsing meaninglessness.

Schubert Ogden's comments on all this are of interest partly because he is concerned, in his essay on "The Reality of God," to find a middle way between traditional supernaturalism and naturalism (or in other terms, between classical theism and atheism). He considers that for various reasons the old supernaturalism is incoherent; but on the other hand does not say anything to our limiting questions. He is seeking a third way, lying beyond the positions which are commonly and rather barrenly opposed to one another.

His argument has two main phases. One is to see the primary use or function of the word "God" as being to refer to

> . . . the objective ground in reality itself of our ineradicable confidence in the final worth of our existence. It lies in the nature of this basic confidence to affirm that the real whole of which we experience ourselves to be parts is such as to be worthy of, and thus itself to evoke, that very confidence. The word "God," then, provides the designation for whatever it is about the experienced whole that calls forth and justifies our original and inescapable trust . . .[5]

The second phase of the argument is to present an account of God and the world in terms of process theology: he is thought of (in accordance with suggestions elicited from Alfred North Whitehead, Charles Hartshorne, and others) as a living and even growing God, related to the universe of other beings somewhat as the human self is related to the body. The point of this last suggestion is that if God is conceived classically as unchanging, etc., then it is hard to see how our moral and other endeavors have any real meaning for him. Only if what we do makes a difference to God, does God stand as the answer to our questions about the worth of life and of moral endeavor. So God must be changing; and further he must be seen as himself woven into the very fabric of the world which we experience, not standing apart in another world, leading a parallel existence, so to say. (It is incidentally interesting, though Ogden is unaware of the point, I suspect, that the Indian theologian Ramanuja, of the eleventh and twelfth centuries, A.D., expounded a very similar doctrine of the relation between God and the world.)

The first phase of the argument is the more immediately relevant to the present discussion, though the second phase serves to indicate the place of Ogden's thinking in current attempts to re-create Christian theology. The first phase involves Ogden in the claim that in fact our response to the threat of meaninglessness has to be positive: even suicide, for him, is seen as intended as a significant and positive act, which itself would be barren of ultimate meaning without some kind of confidence about the ultimate nature of the world. Yet it could be replied that there are those who would reject this rather optimistic view. What of Jean-Paul Sartre, for instance, who can say, "All existing things are born for no reason, continue through weakness and die by accident . . . It is meaningless that we are born; it is meaningless that we die"? [6] Let us return later to this point. But in the meantime, let us go along with Ogden's claim that ultimate confidence is inescapable, and is indeed implicit in all our activities. There yet remain difficulties about his account.

One of these is the problem of how Ogden's view relates to actual religions. He regards them as so many more or less self-conscious attempts to understand the original self-confidence we possess. They thus provide various symbolic forms through which we can reaffirm our existential faith in ultimate meaningfulness. Now this can hardly be a full explanation of the nature of religions, for one has to account for the *variety* of symbolic forms. Further, can one express one's self-confidence without attempting to say something *true* about the world? Is not Ogden's own process theology not intended somehow as a correct delineation of reality which will *justify* the self-confidence? For instance, he appeals to the way our actions must somehow make a difference to God. But if they didn't? Then the confidence in the ultimate worth of what we do would or ought to break down. If, then, something has to be *true* to justify the confidence, we can easily conceive that none of the religious accounts are true, and that maybe therefore we should abandon ourselves to accepting meaninglessness.

A way out of this objection might be to treat the religious accounts as *merely* symbolic and expressive. They are not so much justifications of our self-confidence as expressions of it in mythic, symbolic form. But then, how do they help us to accept the tragedies, etc., which threaten us? How do they play an existential role in helping us to go beyond despair and to have the heart to pursue our duties, etc.? If they merely express my confidence, then they simply drop away when I do not have it. As symbolic forms, religions would have to do more: they would have to evoke the confidence as well as express it. But this implies that I can fail to have the confidence in ultimate meaning, despite Ogden's claim that it is somehow inescapable. We can therefore present him with a dilemma. Either I have this self-confidence inescapably, in which case the limiting questions have no impact on me—they represent no kind of threat—or I am liable to lose it, in which case a position like Sartre's becomes possible. In the one case, religion does not move one; in the other case it may be false.

In any event, it is doubtful whether it is enough to look on the role of religion here just in terms of theology or symbolic forms. As we saw in the first Chapter, religion is a rich and complex thing, and it would be relevant to consider the relationship between limiting questions about conduct and, for instance, worship and contemplation. Thus in actual theistic religions, moral endeavor is seen as related to worship, even a mode of it—by doing good I am rendering praise to the Creator, the sacrifices of God are a broken spirit, etc. A lot of Buddhist meditation is concerned with rousing an existential awareness of the transitoriness of things. Hence it would be as important to relate questions of living meaning to religious practices as it would be to relate them to religious ideas. And yet how does it help, at the limits of moral questioning, to see my fulfilment of a duty as a case of obedience to and praise of God?

Well, somehow I am given an extra reason, but not strictly a moral one. If I try to turn it into a moral one, see what happens. I am told that it is my duty to do this duty, because God demands it, and I have a duty to God (say, because I owe everything to him). But my question now moves on a step: but why fulfil my duty to God? It has the same limiting character as my original question. It recurs when all the moral answers have been given. This point is of course related to the thesis that moral discourse is autonomous, i.e., it cannot be derived from something else, such as the will of God, for we still need a moral reason for obeying the will of God. So seeing my duty as a form of worship might be relevant to the limiting question situation, since it does not so much give a moral answer, but provides a different way of looking at the duty (and morality as a whole). Religion in this sense lies beyond morality, though it incorporates it by seeing it in religious terms. But my sense of the worth of morality can only be reinforced or reexpressed if I am moved by worship itself—if it, that is, is a central value in my life. For if it is not, if it is "meaningless," empty, then its meaninglessness and emptiness will simply transfer itself to the morality I am trying to justify. It is rather as though someone were to say to me: "Well at least do this for the sake of your children," when I do not love my children.

Put another way: if my commitment to worship is liable to break down, religion does not provide a certain ground or milieu for overcoming the threat of loss of value induced by meditative, limiting questions. But then what does "break down" mean here? It may be that in fact men's commitment to worship can break down; just as it seems that in fact men can lack the self-confidence of which Ogden speaks. But perhaps they ought not to; i.e., there is something irrational or self-contradictory about such a breakdown or failure. This seems to be the basis of Ogden's position—that the very idea of treating the world as absurd is absurd. Commenting on Albert Camus' *The Myth of Sisyphus*, he wrote: "But, intriguing as the notion of the absurd hero doubtless is, it can hardly define a real possibility, whether for thought or for existential choice. If all our actions are in principle absurd, the act of heroically resisting their absurdity must also be absurd." [7] Likewise, it might be that inherent in worship is the notion that its Object *necessarily* exists, so that to begin by worshipping and then to think it absurd is wrongly to suppose that God either exists or does not. God is not a contingent being. This thought forms a starting point for an interesting treatment of the problem of God's necessity by J. N. Findlay, in a celebrated article reprinted in Flew and MacIntyre's *New Essays in Philosophical Theology* and entitled "Can God's Existence be Disproved?" [8] (It happens, by the way, that Findlay's position has shifted a bit since he wrote this essay, but this does not detract from the interest of what he there says.)

Discussing the nature of worship, he writes: "And hence we are led on irresistibly to demand that our religious object should have an *unsurpassable* supremacy along all avenues, that it should tower *infinitely* above all other objects." [9] Out of this demand Findlay elicits others, culminating in the most stringent one of all:

> There must, in short, be no conceivable alternative to an existence properly termed "divine": God must be wholly inescapable . . . whether for thought or reality. And so we are led on insensibly to the barely intelligible notion of a Being in whom Essence and Existence lose their separateness. And all that the great

medieval thinkers really did was to carry such a development to its logical conclusion.[10]

Or, to spell this last point out, the Ontological Argument must be right, in principle: that God exists must follow from his nature.

But, and here is the sting in Findlay's article, this conclusion is absurd, a self-contradiction. The idea of necessary existence (for reasons which we shall come to in a moment) is absurd. So God must have a character as object of adoration which entails his non-existence. The self-contradictory just must be false. God cannot exist, precisely because he must! In brief, there is a disproof of God's existence.

The reasons for saying that necessary existence is an absurd notion go back to Kant's criticism of the Ontological Argument. Material and explanations of Kant's argument can be found in my *Historical Selections in the Philosophy of Religion*.[11] But in more recent times the criticism has been put in a more linguistic way than that in which Kant expressed it. In brief, the criticism is that *necessity* is properly a property of propositions (statements, etc.) and not of things. Thus to say "God's existence is necessary" is to say "The statement 'God exists' is necessarily true." But how can a statement be necessarily true? As we saw in an earlier Chapter such necessity comes about from the meanings of the terms employed. Thus "A bachelor is unmarried" is necessarily true, because being unmarried is part of the meaning of the term *bachelor*. Necessary truth then arises out of linguistic convention, not from the way the world is. But in saying something does or does not exist we are saying something about the way the world is, not about the meanings of words. This is one reason why the word "exists" and its relatives ("existence," etc.) have special logical roles to play. "Existence" does not stand for a property of things. It is not a quality, like redness. (This is why we can sensibly say that some tigers are not striped, but cannot sensibly say that some tigers do not exist.) In short, existence cannot be a quality necessarily contained in the nature of God: or (to put it better, and linguistically) "existence" cannot be part of the meaning of "God." So then, the notion of necessary existence is incoherent. If the concept of God entails necessary existence, the concept of God is itself incoherent. If it is incoherent, then any proposition containing the term *God* must be necessarily false. Because God must exist, on Findlay's argument, he cannot.

Findlay's argument is not, however, a disproof of actual objects of religious worship. For worshippers may not go so far as to make the stringent demand that "true religion" according to Findlay must make. Worshippers may be satisfied with a less exalted being. But if so that Being might not exist. He is contingent. Consequently there is always not only a psychological but a rational possibility for such adherents of a faith to cease to worship. That is, it does not involve a kind of contradiction to suppose that after all the Object of worship does not exist. But in this case the absolute certainty which worship might have afforded out of its own substance does not exist, and so it cannot serve as the means of expressing the inescapable confidence about the ultimate meaning of moral action, etc., which we were discussing earlier. By another route we have come to see that Ogden's self-confidence is not inescapable. There remains a point to claims about the inherent absurdity of human existence.

Before, however, moving on from this point we should be clear about what it means to say that absolute certainty is not possible. I am not denying that psychologically it is possible for people to possess a faith which nothing will move: they are certain of what they believe, in this sense. But there is a distinction between what can happen psychologically and the rational basis for belief. What is being claimed here is only that from the point of view of a rational or philosophical evaluation of the issues, it is logically possible (i.e., it is not inconsistent to hold) that any justification of ultimate meaning, whether mediated through belief about the world or through worship, can be mistaken. In so far as rational considerations enter into the way we feel and think (for we are trained to match our attitudes to reality and to the logic of the situation), the recognition of the possibility of error in the justification of our self-confidence about the ultimate worthwhileness of our activities will tend to infect our psychological dispositions. Thus if the argument here used is correct, absolute psychological certainty may be eroded by rational considerations.

But a word of warning is needed about what counts as rational. I am not here wanting to imply that cerebration is all. It is not wise to think of rationality as merely an intellectual matter, even if it is common to do so. For what is reasonable and unreasonable, and what sort of reasons count and what do not—these questions are to do with the subject-matter and with the aspect of life we are considering. It is most important that we should not make one kind of category-mistake: of failing to see the true nature of the type of concepts which we are dealing with in (say) religion. We argued in the first Chapter that to understand religious concepts we should see them in their living milieu. This means that we have to see them in the context of, among other things, such activities as worship and contemplation. To treat the question of God as though it is a question about the existence of a First Cause only is to make such a category-mistake. It is to see religion under the guise of a simply metaphysical system. Consequently, the "rational considerations" which may erode absolute certainty are not just intellectual, but have to do with the fabric of religious faith and the nature of living. This should no doubt be clear from the very fact that Findlay's argument was an attempt to explicate not so much some theoretical demand of reason, as the inner logic of worship (about which, however, he may have been wrong).

It cannot then be said that a religious answer to the limiting questions provides an unthreatened certainty that the values challenged by those limiting questions are somehow conserved in the ultimate meaningfulness of existence. Indeed, it may be that the attempt at certainty here simply rids the questions of their force. If they are bound to get the right answer, we forget after a while to ask them. It may, therefore, also be that we should reject the goals set by Ogden and Findlay (inescapable self-confidence and ontological necessity) as appropriate to religious faith but inconsistent with the very challenges set by the limiting questions and situations, and therefore with the possibility of any real force in the religious answers. For that matter, faith may have to be a bit blind: we do not have faith in what we already know certainly to be so.

The limiting questions about morals described by Toulmin represent one kind, as we have seen, of meditative ways of seeing the possibility of meaninglessness (of the loss of value, to use another phrase that has figured in the discussion). The very fact that one goes on asking the question of why one should be moral after all the moral answers have been given indicates that here the whole enterprise has begun to seem pointless. If religion gives an "answer" it is through weaving moral action into a wider framework. But the nature of this framework is not yet sufficiently clear.

One aspect of this placing of morality and other values in a wider framework is the connection of them with worship (and so in general with the concepts employed in worship) or with other aspects of the religious life. (Worship, however, is a familiar example for those brought up in or in the vicinity of the theistic religions, so I shall concentrate on it here.) The fact that morality can be assumed under worship indicates one manner in which religion is not just an activity which is part of life, but has connections with the rest of life. Thus in addressing oneself to the *mysterium tremendum et fascinans* (see Chapter I) one can see the threats of death, whether individual or collective, and the limiting questions of value, in a new light. Under one aspect, as *mysterium*, the Object of worship, and so of moral action, is incomprehensible: but the limiting situation offers no hope of an ordinary "this-worldly" explanation. Further, as *mysterium*, the process of worship has to do with changing, not with learning—with undergoing an experience, rather than gaining information, etc. (see above, p. 71): so too the answer to a limiting situation has to do with giving people heart, inspiring them, even in depressing circumstances. As *tremendum*, the Object of worship creates awe and humility. The humility ties in with the selflessness which the pursuit of duty and joint enterprises demands; and the fearful side of divinity reminds us that death too comes from God, as well as life. Hence there is an ambiguity in the divine presence which does not allow the challenge and the anguish in the questions and circumstances to wither away in a pious optimism. Yet as *fascinans*, the Object of worship is the supreme, moving joy for us. This supreme value somehow overarches and subsumes the lesser values which we pursue outside the context of adoration. In this way, these other pursuits too can become a mode of adoration (so marriage, for instance, becomes, in Christian terminology, a sacrament).

This, in brief, is a delineation of the way in which a central aspect of religion can (so to say) reinforce the values of ordinary life. Moral endeavor, the joint enterprises we engage in, the moments of death and birth and marriage—these are solemnised and consecrated and thus "validated" by reference to the worship of the Holy. Failure and suffering as well as success and joy can be subsumed under the sacrifices and celebrations of religion. But worship of the Holy can only perform these functions of "justifying" what we elsewhere do if it grips us—if, that is, we see it as a moving experience in itself. If my love of ballet withers, that does not necessarily affect the rest, for I do not justify the value of other things by reference to ballet. But the religious way of life seeks to focus other activities on the central value of worship (etc.): it superimposes the Holy on other values. If the power of the Holy to move us fades, then this overarching, meaning-giving function of faith will break down.

Another aspect of the placing of moral and other values in a wider framework is through doctrines and myths, such as those of eternal life, immortality, and resurrection. Thus in the Christian tradition, man is placed in relation to the eternal, and has the promise from God of eternal life; man is also given a "future" (so that he has hopes that his ongoing enterprises can be consummated at the "end" of history) through the promise of the kingdom and the resurrection of the body. This aspect is nearer what Toulmin and Ogden seem to mean, in thinking that religion somehow offers heart and consolation in the boundary situations of life, and the trust that after all our confidence in the worthwhileness of our endeavors is not misplaced. But it is hard to see how the myths and doctrines can function unless the individual thinks of himself as able to enter into relationship with the source of these hopes of immortality and consummation. This implies that he has to look to the manifestations of the religious ultimate here and now: in short he has to look towards the life of religion (and thus to worship, etc.). In this way the second aspect ties in with the first, and one sees how a merely metaphysical account of the meaning of existence fails to take account of the way in which *religion* may give meaning to life. But then this implies in turn that *this* sort of meaning for existence is not inescapable, since it is possible to reject religion and religions.

But even if there is the possibility of rejecting the religious justification of values (such as it is—for we already have the values: as we argued earlier, morality is, for instance, autonomous and so is not derivable from religious belief), the present discussion may show why it is that religion at least functions as an answer to the questions arising at the boundaries of life. It may not be the only answer; but it is one (or to be more precise, it is a range of answers, for the religions give different pictures of man's place in the world and of the central values that can animate his existence, even in conditions of stress and anxiety). This accounts for the fact that much of present-day Christian theology takes existentialism as a starting-point, since existentialism concerns itself much with questions of the meaning of life and the threat of death, etc.

The fact that people encounter these meditative and actual threats to their values and so are susceptible to the onset of "meaninglessness" is one reason for making religion a live option. But it can only serve to avert the threat of meaninglessness, if our account is correct, if the path that it offers and the values that it enshrines in practice are moving, impressive, beguiling. Of course also people have to feel that it is true. But if what it offers by way of relationship to the religious ultimate does not ring a bell in human hearts, it offers no consolation for the loss of other values. For this reason we can begin to answer an earlier question which we left: is the life of the Chinese revolutionary somehow more meaningful than that of the Tuscan peasant?

First, threats to meaningfulness are not just meditative, but also actual (as with the man who loses his wife); thus we have to see meaningfulness not just as a general problem, but to do with individuals. There is no *a priori* prescription to be followed here. And if, as we have just said, religion has to ring a bell—well, its success in doing this is not just a function of its own institutions and atmosphere, but of the hearts it has to move as well. Second, religion can provide a focus under which piecemeal and varying pursuits of individual and joint enterprises can be subsumed. Thus Brother Lawrence saw his daily activities in the light of service and prayer: but he did not see himself as participating in a big historical movement. The sense of taking part in a big movement is not the only way in which one may gain the feeling of the enhanced significance of one's activities. Third, meaningfulness is not the same as right meaningfulness. It is quite possible that religious and other justifications of values and modes of dealing with the threat of death, etc., are mistaken. Even if the Chinese revolutionary's existence turned out to be more meaningful, it could still be directed towards wrong ends, etc.

To sum up the discussion so far. Questions about the living meaning of existence broadly have to do with threats of the loss of values in personal and collective life. Such a loss of value can occur naturally, through the shattering of a person's fabric of interests, enjoyments and so on; but it can also occur as a result of reflective meditation on boundary situations, such as death and the possibility of total human destruction and demise. Connectedly, we can press moral questioning beyond the limits where it is possible to give a rational moral answer: such limiting questions express a desire for reassurance about the point of being moral. Religion can provide such reassurance in as much as morality is seen not only as morality but as a form of the religious life. But this reassurance can, of course, only work if religion itself is valued: is itself seen as having point. The discussion indicates that to enter into the full meaning of a religious system, it is necessary to appreciate its role in giving such reassurance and "validation" to moral and other values. Or, to put the matter in different jargon, religion has to be seen as existentially significant. There are two ways therefore in which a religion can (while retaining sentential meaning in its claims) begin to lose living meaning. One way results from a fading of people's absorption and interest in the practices of religion (such as worship)—they begin to seem "pointless." Another way is the result of a gulf between a religion's practices and the existential concerns of men in a given milieu. A church can then become like a cricket club—absorbing for the members, but not linked up with (as we say) real (i.e. the rest of) life. Still, in order to enter into a religion imaginatively, to understand it, one needs to see at least how it *could* have living meaning in the wider context. This is one reason why problems of the meaning of religious statements cannot finally be divorced from problems of the meaning of life. It is also a reason why the person who loses faith can easily think of religious utterances as no longer being meaningful: well, they remain meaningful, in fact, but they have lost living meaning for him.

It may be noted that the account we have given corresponds to a feature of functionalist theory in the sociology of religion. Thus

Thomas F. O'Dea (*The Sociology of Religion,*) in expounding functionalism writes:

> As inherent characteristics of the human condition, contingency and powerlessness bring men face-to-face with situations in which established techniques and mundane social prescriptions display a total insufficiency for providing "mechanisms" for adjustment. They confront men with "breaking points" in the socially structured round of daily behavior. As "breaking beyond" ordinary experience, they raise questions which can find an answer only in some kind of "beyond" itself. At these "breaking points", what Max Weber has called "the problem of meaning" arises in the severest and most poignant manner. Why should I die? Why should a loved one die, and in unfulfilled youth? . . . Such questions demand meaningful answers. If they are found to be without meaning, the value of institutionalized goals and norms is undermined. How can morale be maintained when . . . death, the ultimate disappointment, strikes at our utter defenselessness in the end? [12]

But though religion may have such a social role of maintaining morale, etc., it is not wise to jump to the conclusion that its function explains its genesis. It is equally an open question, which we shall discuss later on, as to whether the psychological functions of religion justify a psychological explanation of religion. These are open questions for various reasons. First, there are very different kinds of religions, and their variations cannot be given a monolithic sociological or psychological explanation. Second, a sociological or psychological explanation of the genesis of religion would have to establish that it exhaustively dealt with all aspects of religion. What if the numinous experience, for instance, is something which enables us to perceive an aspect of reality not accessible in other ways? Third, it is by no means correct to think of religious beliefs and practices as justifying existing social norms, etc. They often challenge them (hence the importance of Max Weber's work, in pointing to the dynamic, causative role of religion in social and economic change).

Indeed, the fact that the Object of worship is liable to be conceived as possessing eternity and promising eternal life, beyond the vicissitudes and contingencies of mundane existence, means that religious values are as much liable to challenge social conventions as to validate them. Earthly goals come, so to say, under a higher scrutiny. This is one reason for the "world-denying" element that keeps recurring in religious history.

There is something of this, for instance, in the LSD cult which has developed in recent years. Here is a substance which its users consider to give them a kind of window on reality, through which one sees something deeper and more significant than that which is given in everyday experience. It provides a living meaning which ties in with social protest and withdrawal from the goals which ordinary social success demands. The movement is thus simultaneously (like much religion) one whose central experience is held to justify itself and a means of social criticism and protest. All this is not to say that the movement has the right values or that LSD stands comparison with the practices of the great religions in bringing people to a knowledge of some transcendental truth. It may be a false, foolish, and dangerous cult, just as some religions are liable to be false, foolish, and dangerous. It is not our present concern to argue these questions, but only to illustrate ways in which the transcendental values and central experience of religious cults can themselves be as much a challenge to existing conventions as a means of validating them.

The first three Chapters have attempted to give a sketch of the nature of religious systems and of problems connected with understanding them. It can be stressed again that this understanding must involve a kind of imaginative participation in religious practice, experience, and relevance to the limiting situations and questions which have to do with living meaning. It is implicit in the argument of this Chapter that religion is not derivable from the problems of living meaning, but rather presents a way or ways of seeing them. So the understanding of religious relevance, in this sense, is only one aspect of understanding religious life and concepts. But I hope enough has been said to show that it is not possible to deal with questions of religious truth as though religious propositions are simply metaphysical.

We can therefore rid ourselves of the illusion conveyed by much philosophical treatment of religious claims that they can be assessed in a merely speculative way. We must obey the rule that concepts should be seen in context. This context is not just linguistic, but extra-linguistic. Religious concepts therefore need to be seen in the context of the forms of religious life—and even more broadly, in as much as religions provide one set of answers to what we have called problems of living meaning. It is a cheerful sign that quite a lot of recent philosophy of religion tries in such ways to be realistic about religious concepts, just as the philosophy of science has rid itself of an earlier tendency to think out the nature of science from the armchair, instead of looking at what scientists actually do and at the actual fabric of scientific theories.

But meaning, as we have noted, is not to be separated utterly from truth. It is now time to turn to questions of religious truth. It is not my intention to try to show what (if any) religion is true and what (if any) is false. The task is not that of apologetics. Rather we must look at the kinds of arguments, reasons, evidences and considerations which are to be employed in settling the substantive questions. Still, at one level it will be necessary to look at the validity of some arguments, for instance the classical attempts to prove the existence of God. It is to this extent necessary to take sides. But I do not think it is the primary job of the philosophy of religion to defend or attack theism (or any other form of religion). Since, however, one does not wish to divide labor over-precisely, there is no great harm in a philosophically trained person's going in for such apologetics.

Notes

1. Gilbert Ryle, *The Concept of Mind* (New York: Barnes & Noble, 1950).
2. Stephen Toulmin, *An Examination of the Place of Reason in Ethics* (Cambridge, Eng.: Cambridge University Press, 1950–1960).
3. Schubert M. Ogden, *The Reality of God, and Other Essays* (New York: Harper & Row, 1966).
4. Toulmin, *op. cit.*, p. 219.
5. Schubert M. Ogden, "The Reality of God," in Ogden, *op. cit.*, p. 37.

6. Ronald Hepburn, in Antony Flew and Alasdair MacIntyre, eds., *New Essays in Philosophical Theory* (New York: Macmillan), p. 140.
7. Schubert M. Ogden, "The Reality of God," in Ogden, *op. cit.*, p. 41.
8. J. N. Findlay, "Can God's Existence be Disproved?" in Antony Flew and Alasdair MacIntyre (eds.), *New Essays in Philosophical Theology* (New York: Macmillan), pp. 47 ff.
9. *Ibid.*, p. 51.
10. Findlay, *op. cit.*, p. 52.
11. Ninian Smart, *Historical Selections in the Philosophy of Religion* (New York: Harper & Row, 1962), pp. 248 ff.
12. Thomas F. O'Dea, *The Sociology of Religion* (Englewood Cliffs, N. J.: Prentice-Hall), p. 5.

Chapter Four ❧

❧ ❧ ❧ On the Idea of Revealed Truth

It would be in line with a realistic approach to problems about religious truth to answer the question, "On what basis can the truth of a religion be established?" by saying, "On authority." For is it not the case in practice that religious people appeal to revelation or some other authority? It is not as if they have worked out the truths incorporated in their faith from personal experience. Such personal experience of a religious nature that they may have had is on the contrary nurtured in the milieu of a tradition and a community, with the attendant practices, such as worship, which make up the daily life of the tradition. In approaching God, people already accept a tradition about him. It may be that in some way or other personal experience of the Holy can confirm the authoritative tradition, so that the adherent can say, "I know that my redeemer liveth." But it is still in essence (it would seem) by appeal to authority that the believer establishes the truth of his faith.

Yet this seems a somewhat brutish method of establishing truth. Do I simply believe something because someone tells me it is true? Have I no freedom to criticise? Do we not in fact arrive at the truth not by simple acceptance, but by testing what is proposed, by experimenting, by using our judgment? And is this way not incompatible with a simple appeal to authority? Given the previous analysis of religion, it seems that there is a dilemma.

On the one hand, religion has to be seen in its living milieu. That living milieu presents the religious ultimate as something given. Consequently, the descriptions of the religious ultimate within a tradition are themselves given. Thus it seems inescapable that there are claimed truths which are simply accepted on authority by those who participate in such a community. On the other hand, truth does not depend on mere say-so. It has to be arrived at critically. There is a tension between religion as it is and truth (and thus belief) as it ought to be. This seems a powerful reason for rejecting religion, for truth is no respecter of persons, still less of institutions and traditions.

Yet it is implicit in the notion that we arrive at truth by criticism that there is something to criticise. Earlier we noted that falsifiability came to replace verifiability as the criterion of meaningfulness, the reason being that there are ways of showing something to be false when corresponding ways of showing it to be true are absent. Thus the philosopher of science Karl Popper has put up a strong case for saying that the definition of a scientific hypothesis (as distinguished from some metaphysical speculation) is that it is capable of being disproved. The cosmologist Herman Bondi has used this criterion as a partial defence of the Steady State theory in cosmology (see p. 56), since it makes predictions about the distribution of galaxies, etc., and thus sticks its neck out sufficiently to risk its being chopped off by counter-evidence—the mark of a fruitful hypothesis. On this view, the survival of theories which stick their necks out in the face of attempts to disprove them on experimental and observational evidence is the chief sign of their truth. But also on this view, we do not need to worry too much where the hypotheses come from. They do not need to be (and in fact they cannot be) built up meticulously from what is given in immediate experience and observation. They necessarily go beyond what we already know. They are hazards against nature. If nature rejects them, they are shown to be false. In brief, one begins from what is given not so much in experience as in the scientific imagination. There is something thrown up there which one can set about criticising. Though this picture of scientific method cannot for various reasons be regarded as completely adequate, it has more than a grain of truth. To put the matter crudely:

science is a result of the interplay between concepts and experience.
If we try to derive all the concepts from experience there is no
interplay. So it is not absurd to begin from something given in (so
to say) the religious imagination. That something is constituted by
authoritative traditions.

But, it will be replied, there is a difference of vital importance
between the two cases. On the one hand science is explicitly self-
critical and thus does not present hypotheses in an authoritative
manner. It is true that the reputation of a particular scientist may
add weight to the hazards that he makes. It is true that there can
easily arise even in science a climate of opinion which constitutes a
sort of unreflected-upon authority constricting the possibilities enter-
tained by those engaged in the field. But in principle science is
hostile to these personal and social factors. Its self-criticism in
principle transcends appeal to personal or social authority. On the
other hand it seems that religion depends very much on who and
what community asserts things. It is bound up with personal and
social authority.

It is true that there is often a high degree of conformism in
religious communities and traditions (though it is worth noting too
how often in the history of religions unorthodoxies have emerged
either explicitly in the guise of unorthodoxies or in the guise of
orthodoxies: religions certainly change, whatever theories may be
held of the unalterability of their central truths, etc.). It may be
that the conformism has to do with more than truth: or rather, that
the beliefs of a community are more than attempts at delineating
reality, but also in essence form part of the constitution of the
community. Their authority, that is, may in part be like that of the
United States Constitution—binding, even if (within the terms of
the Constitution) alterable. The fact that religious traditions are
embedded in social institutions, such as the Church, may mean that
personal and social authority plays a more central role than in the
more diffuse institutions of a scientific discipline.

But it is not in any case possible to evaluate the notion of authority
in religion without seeing in particular how it expresses itself. One
important expression is in the idea of revealed truth. This in turn is
seen in various ways. Let us confine our discussion here for the most

part to the Christian tradition, where revealed truth has typically to do with the Bible. This is seen as the main source of truth about the nature of God, man, and salvation.

It happens that a number of positions on this question have been taken up, both classically and in recent times. For instance, it is thought by many Christians that the Bible is inerrant, and that one can deduce truths about God, etc., from the propositions contained in it. This view has been called the "propositional view of revelation," though I prefer to call it the "deductivist view." This position can be held in such a way that the Bible is the *only* source of truths about God, etc.; but it can also be joined with the conviction that one can gain knowledge of God outside the Bible, for example through natural theology (this being, of course, the classical Roman Catholic standpoint). The two views can be labelled "exclusive deductivism" and "non-exclusive deductivism" respectively.

Alternatively, there is the view that one cannot simply deduce truths about God, etc., from the sentences of the Bible because the latter are fallible and to some degree dated. This is the major view among Protestant theologians today, and also has many Catholic adherents. It might be dubbed "inductivism," for in order to arrive at truths about God, etc., one has to go through the words of the Bible to what they represent, making allowances for the circumstances and thought-forms of the writers of the various parts of scripture. Revelation is thus considered to be the manifestation of God's nature through his acts in history and in particular in Christ. Inductivism, again, can be joined with the view that there are other (less important) avenues to knowledge about God, or with the view that there are none such. The inductivist view has seemed to be forced on reflective Christians by the progress made in the application of historical methods to the Biblical material in the last century and a half, and by the impact of scientific discoveries or theories, such as the Theory of Evolution, which prevent Christians from taking *Genesis* literally, but rather as a mythic representation of the dependence of the world on God. This awareness of the mythic character of much Biblical writing has culminated in the demythologisation movement associated with the work of Rudolf Bultmann. The aim is to restate the Gospel in such a way that the older mythic forms are replaced by ideas conveying a similar force in the thought of today (for how can *we* any longer seriously participate in the mythological thought-forms of the New Testament writers? We belong to a different age).

It should be noted that the rejection, by many evangelical Protestants, of natural theology and in general of "natural" means of knowing truths about God rests more on religious presuppositions than on detailed scepticism about the proofs and evidences of God's existence which have been offered in the history of philosophical and theological thought. The reason rather is that knowledge of God is not speculative and theoretical, but is bound up with salvation. Any knowledge of God is, so to say, saving knowledge. But only God has the power to save. Consequently, only God can give knowledge of himself. It is only through his self-manifestation—through revelation—that one can know him.

This position is important, for it gets to the root of some vital problems in the philosophy of religion. It has its most powerful expression in the writings of Karl Barth, who took an inductivist rather than a deductivist view of revelation, but at the same time belongs to the main stream of evangelical Protestantism (which in recent times has tended to be deductivist and even often literalist in its treatment of the scripture).

What is the reason for saying that knowledge of God essentially has to do with salvation? And what is the reason for saying that only God can save? The first question can be answered by reference to our earlier discussion about the significance of religious concepts. The knowledge of God is not something theoretical, for two reasons. One is that such knowledge involves an acquaintance with God as manifested. (It is knowing God, rather than hearsay about him.) Another is that the knowledge to count as "true knowledge" must involve a change in the knower—i.e., the Object of worship makes an existential impact upon the worshipper, etc. In the terminology of Rudolf Otto, to repeat, God is the *mysterium tremendum et fascinans*; so I have not truly found him if I do not find him to be *tremendum et fascinans*, if I do not acknowledge his power and grace. Such sentiments lie behind the idea that knowledge of God is saving knowledge, though I have stated them rather more widely than would Barth, who is confined in his exegesis to the material supplied by the Bible, and by Paul's epistle to the Romans in particular. (It is, however, unwise to generalize about Barth, whose thought continually evolved through the many and still unending volumes of his magisterial *Church Dogmatics*. Also, Barth was much impressed and distressed at the way his liberal, non-exclusivist, theological teachers before World War I in Germany succumbed to the Kaiser's ideology, and even more pained, and rightly, with the manner in which many Christians, so-called, followed Hitler: he therefore wished to keep the Gospel uncontaminated by human ideology so that it could present a clean and powerful challenge to the values of fallen men. Hence his exclusivism about revelation.)

The reason why saving knowledge must itself come from God and not from the unaided reasonings of men depends, as we have seen, on the principle that only God can save. If we simplify the notion of salvation to mean the acquisition of holiness, then it is not hard to see that (at least on monotheistic principles) salvation must come from God. There is only one Holy Being, and anything else which is holy derives its holiness from him. Hence I can only derive my salvation from God, and it is only from God that one can get knowledge of God. Of course, it could be answered by those who believe in a natural knowledge of God through reasoning that God gave men the capacity to reason about him, so that such knowledge too comes from God and is thus maybe saving knowledge. I shall revert to this point later, in connection with the so-called proofs of the existence of God which classically have been advanced.

The above lines of thought seem to present an acute problem about the criteria of truth in religion. They seem to imply a circularity and closedness in the appeal to authority. It looks like saying: "I know that there is a God by faith; and this faith is true because it is God-given." In terms of a deductivist position, it would look like saying: "I know that there is a God, for his nature and acts are described in the scriptures; and the scriptures are true, because they have been inspired by God." In practice, of course, the appeal to revelation is a good deal more complex than this, and one has to read the scriptures, respond to Christ, etc., in the context of a faith which ties in with worship, the community life, etc. But it is useful for us to consider problems about religious truth in relation to the above impression of closedness.

The above argument has been, as has been mentioned, stated in a rather wider way than that adopted by Barth. It is possible therefore to distinguish between a wider and a narrower sort of closedness. The narrower version is fully-fledged Barthianism, and amounts to the thesis that there are no grounds in human reason or experience for faith, except in the experience of God's word manifested in Christ. There are then no "external" criteria of truth in religion. The wider version also holds that religious truth cannot be established on external grounds, but holds that religion represents a certain realm of experience (say of the Holy) within which the truth may be discovered. This wider version is not tied in advance to the truth of a particular faith. Roughly it is the position of Otto. The wider version has a certain initial plausibility (if we waive for a moment the question of the definition of religion in terms of the Holy); for if religion is a distinctive realm of human experience, how could one hope to say anything about its truth save by attending to that experience? If religious language is a separate form of language, different from other forms of human language, one would surely expect it to have its own "logic." The criteria of truth would be found within the realm of religious language, not outside it. (A sentiment of this sort inspired my *Reasons and Faiths*—an attempt to explore religious language in its own terms, though with reference to a variety of religions.[1])

The narrower version, however, uses the concept of revelation most directly. Let us, through considering, try to lay bare some logical difficulties in the appeal to revelation. And let us first imagine (what in fact is not the case) that there are only two options or proposals for belief (to use a phrase of William Christian's in *Meaning and Truth in Religion*[2]), namely atheism and the Christian revelation. It would then be possible for the Barthian to argue thus: "To take the possibility of religious truth seriously you have to look in the direction in which it manifests itself, namely in the life of Christ, etc., and in the scriptures, which bear witness to it. If you contemplate these, you will see that it is implicit in them that God gives faith and that there is no way of beginning from 'rational' non-revealed premises to arrive at the truth of what is revealed. You are either given faith or you are not." So far there is no inconsistency or inherent absurdity in this appeal.

But in fact we are not only presented with one option other than the rejection of religious faith. Indeed there is an ambiguity about the very idea of the Christian revelation, since the way it is described differs from denomination to denomination, etc., within the Christian tradition. It might look, then, that the Barthian position is only one interpretation of Christianity. Would it not be open to the Roman Catholic to claim an equal validity for *his* interpretation, which implies that in some measure at least it *is* possible to start from non-religious premises and arrive at truths about the existence of God, etc.? To this an *ad hominem* reply could be made, namely: "You, like me, accept the scriptures as a description of God's revelation in Christ; but if you attend seriously to what is said, for instance by Paul, you will see that there can be no transition from human ideas to God: the revelation is absolutely *sui generis*."

But then we are involved in questions of interpretation. These are tricky, delicate, and complex. Still, there are criteria for determining answers in this sphere, so that in principle the Barthian position might be established from the scriptures themselves. Still no inherent absurdity, then, can be discovered in it, though it remains a problem as to why interpretations should vary so much (it could be for disreputable reasons, the tendency of men to try and bend the scriptures, etc., to their own ends; it could also be for more reputable ones—it would, for instance, be in line with the previous discussion of the understanding of religious concepts that a fair amount depends on the sentiments with which and the milieu in which one approaches what is supposedly revealed: some interpretations of scripture, etc., could be simply "wooden" because they were not animated with the right sympathetic imagination, and it could also be that variations in religious experience contributed to the seeing of diverse facets of meaning in revelation).

But the situation is not merely that we are presented with only Christian interpretations of revelation (where the above kind of defence of the Barthian view might work out). There are other faiths entirely, such as Islam and Buddhism. What becomes of the appeal to revelation in such circumstances? The picture is here complicated by the fact that the concept of revelation itself is not universal in religions, so there is not a perfect symmetry between possible revelationist claims on the part of differing faiths. But let us assume for the moment that some exponent of a faith other than

Christianity maintains a position symmetrical with the Barthian one. Or let us formalise a little further and label the two faiths F_1 and F_2: let us suppose that one exponent holds that the religious ultimate manifests itself only in F_1, the other that it does so only in F_2. Is there any sensible way out of this impasse?

There could be if there were some criteria of truth which could be applied to both F_1 and F_2. For instance, the truth of both F_1 and F_2 might partly depend on purely historical questions. In this case historical investigation might be enough to tilt the balance in favor of F_1 rather than F_2. But the essence of the Barthian position at present being considered is that no criteria from outside of revelation can be used to establish its truth. The conflict between F_1 and F_2 therefore takes the form of the F_1 exponent's saying, "F_1 entails the truth of F_1 and so the falsity of F_2," while conversely the exponent of F_2 says, "F_2 entails the truth of F_2 and so the falsity of F_1."

Of course, we have assumed that F_1 and F_2 are different. But might it not turn out that two separate traditions were speaking of the same religious ultimate? This might be so even if the traditions were superficially rather dissimilar, in that religious language is not to be taken too literally, and in as much as the religious ultimate mysteriously transcends the forms under which it manifests itself. It is indeed a fairly popular thesis that all religions somehow point to the same truth. However, it is clear that the *forms* of religion differ, and that the Christian (say) in pointing to Christ is pointing to a manifestation of the religious ultimate not shared by other faiths. There would be no point in the Barthian position if it did not claim fairly specifically that God's revelation is in Christ. It is the very uniqueness of this revelation that makes it a challenge to men's preconceived ideas and shows its divine, transcendent quality.

It is not uncommon for Christian apologists in defending the faith to appeal to the uniqueness of Christianity as if it were somehow a ground for believing it to be true. It takes little reflection, though, to see that uniqueness by itself tells us nothing about the truth or otherwise of a faith. What does it mean to say that something is unique? Just that it has some property or combination of properties not found elsewhere. More particularly, we usually use the term in respect of some relevant property or combination of properties: for instance if I say, "Contrexéville is unique among watering places in having a casino within walking distance of the mineral springs," I am drawing attention to something about Contrexéville relevant to its status as a holiday resort and spa. (There is a slight oddity, unless one is doing a crossword, etc., in saying, "Contrexéville is unique among watering-places in having an *x* as the seventh letter of its name.") To say, then, that Christianity is unique is to claim that it has something different about it, relevant to its status as a faith. It should not surprise us if this were so. But similarly, Islam, Buddhism, and Hinduism, etc., are unique: they are significantly different from one another and from Christianity in respect of the kind of faith and life and beliefs they inspire. Thus it is not by itself a ground for thinking Christianity to be true that it should be unique.

However, one might begin from the assumption (a view at any rate to be found in Barth's writings) that religious ideas and practices are typically human creations: religious beliefs are projections of men's wishes, etc. Then it would be important to note that the Christian revelation was significantly different from other faiths. This might itself be a sign that the Christian revelation does not come from human projections but from God. But here we begin to find a criterion external to revelation itself. For either what counts as a mere projection is determined by revelation itself or there is some set of criteria (e.g., drawn from Freudian psychoanalysis) which is not so determined. In the first case the argument that the uniqueness of revelation is a ground for supposing it not to be a projection crumbles, for all that is being said is that other religions, etc., are false because they do not conform to revelation. It is thus a bare restatement of the kind of thing we referred to earlier: "F_1 entails the truth of F_1 and therefore the falsity of F_2." For the argument, then, to have any force there must be some independent or relatively independent means of finding out whether a religious idea is a projection of human wishes.

In practice it will be difficult to find such criteria. For instance, the idea of an omnipotent punitive Father might perhaps be thought to derive from unconscious wishes; and it could be argued that Christianity transcends such an idea, in the religion of Christ and of love. But Buddhism has no omnipotent punitive Father; so Buddhism transcends the idea even more drastically. But then the notion of nirvana might be thought to have the form of a highly sophisti-

cated death-wish . . . and so on. Not only would the criteria we have
fail to select out a single faith as exempt from wish-fulfilment, but
also the vagueness of the concepts used would allow all sorts of iden-
tifications of projections. Thus it was possible for Erich Fromm to
argue in *The Dogma of Christ and Other Essays* that the doctrine of
the Incarnation, with its idea of two who are yet one, symbolises the
situation in the womb.[3] But what check do we have upon such
speculative psychologisings? On the one hand, they often seem to
bring insight; on the other hand, they are like making out the shapes
of animals in the clouds—the rules are not very precise, to say the
least. Moreover, individuals within a faith and phases of its history
differ largely, and some aspects of a tradition may thus seem like
projections, while others do not. There is always the possibility of
drawing a line between healthy or true religion and the less healthy
and true manifestations of it in practice. Thus Roy S. Lee in *Freud
and Christianity* can argue (and of course he is not alone in this) that
psychoanalytic insights can help us to differentiate between the true
faith and its aberrations and defective expressions.[4] Indeed, Barth
holds, as we saw in the first Chapter, that there is an important distinction between the Gospel and empirical Christianity. For all these
reasons, it is doubtful whether there would be any easy way of elimi-
nating what is false, what are projections of human wishes, from the
truth by independent, non-revelatory means.

What is sauce for the goose is sauce for the gander. If one were to
try to show something radically defective about, say, Islam, it could
always be answered that one should distinguish between the true
message of Muhammad from the false interpretations and slack lives
which have tended to overlay it in the history of the Muslim religion.

Another point emerging from the discussion of uniqueness is this.
Surely it is possible for a faith to be unique in certain respects, while
sharing other relevant characteristics with other faiths. For example,
different religions may hold that God is loving and merciful, even if
they differ in other ways about the way God reveals himself to
mankind, etc. Such similarities, it might be thought, should not be
over-ridden by the unique ones. Allowing them, then, surely it
would follow that if F_1 is true, at least some parts of F_2 must be true.
It is not just a matter of black and white. There are shades of
religious grey. It would not thus be possible to draw such a firm line

as Barth suggests between the Gospel and other faiths, nor would it be easy to condemn other faiths as mere projections of human wishes.

Hendrik Kraemer in *The Christian Message in a Non-Christian World* made a heroic attempt to evade the logic of this argument and to retain the distinction between the Gospel and empirical religion.[5] This book is the one major attempt to apply neo-Protestant principles to the problem of Christianity and other religions. In some measure Kraemer's position was modified in later writings, but this need not here concern us. Kraemer tried to evade the argument by pointing out that religions are organic systems (or as he said "totalitarian" systems—in view of the other connotations of this term I prefer the word "organic"). In the first Chapter we tried to show how religious ideas are woven into religious life and practice; but further, the system or scheme of ideas to be found in a religion are organic, in the sense that the different ideas affect each other's significance. An analogy might be paintings. A patch of red in painting A may have quite a different impact and significance from a patch of red in painting B, because of what respectively surrounds and accompanies the two patches. In one painting it may be the sail of a Thames barge; in the other it may be blood coming from a carcase. So likewise superficially similar ideas in religion may take on quite different significances because of their respective contexts. For instance, the idea of God in Christianity has suffered a sea-change in comparison with its analogue in Judaism, because of the Incarnation. Given such an organic interpretation of religions, it is possible for Kraemer to argue that the supposed points of similarity between religions, and between religions and the Gospel, are not points of similarity at all. It is therefore not possible to conclude that if F_1 is true at least some elements of F_2 must be.

A difficulty with this defence of Barthian closedness is that it appears to destroy the basis for saying that the Christian faith itself as empirically manifested resembles the Gospel. For if it does somehow reflect the Gospel, then there is no reason in principle for a rigid adherence to the thesis that different organic systems cannot properly be compared. The defence also raises the question of what it is that religious truth is predicated of. It would seem that one could not speak of the truth of individual doctrines, but only of the system of ideas as a whole. This would seem to take the idea of organicness to an unacceptable extreme.

For it certainly looks as if some religious propositions can be detached and treated separately, e.g., the proposition that Jesus died on Calvary. It could be replied that such historical statements can so be isolated and treated piecemeal, but not the mythic and doctrinal ramifications which give these historical statements their specially religious significance. Thus Jesus' death on Calvary only takes on a meaning for faith in the light of the claim that Jesus was Christ and Son of God and that by his death he atoned for men's sins and brought men back to the possibility of true communion with God, etc.

Now although it is convenient for certain purposes to differentiate between the historical and the mythic-doctrinal sides of Christian affirmations about revelation and salvation, it does not square with the organic thesis to escape the objection in the above way. For if it be true that the significance of (say) the idea of Creation is affected by belief in Christ, it must be affected by the belief in an incarnate Christ. But the latter did certain things and died in a certain way. His biography is part of the mythic dimension of the Christian faith. Consequently, one cannot just detach the mythic-doctrinal aspect from the historical. It would seem as if two things are simultaneously true: we must treat religious systems as organic, including their historical beliefs; and we must treat parts of these systems (e.g., the historical claims) as true or false by themselves. This points to an organicism which is not extreme. It seems reasonable to think of the various elements of a religious system as units which can be treated in a preliminary way as independent. In further exploring their significance we relate them to the other elements, and so on. This indeed is a task of theology within a given religion, to show how the different parts of belief affect each other's significance and hang together. The extreme doctrine of organicism on the other hand would have to involve a kind of entailment between different beliefs, and this is too strong a relation to describe the mutual interplay of beliefs within a system. An important part, however, is played by a weaker relation, which might be called "suggestion," whereby one belief is seen to be a natural adjunct of another. (This point is explored in R. C. Coburn's article "The Concept of God" and in my own *Reasons and*

Faiths.) [6] But even on this weaker view of organicism, it is not quite right to think of elements in the system as true or false just like that. Allowance has to be made for deeper levels of meaning arising from the way these elements are affected by the rest of the system. There is a case therefore for using some such locution as "approximately true" to predicate of elements of a system of beliefs.

From the point of view of the less extreme view of the organic nature of religious systems, the attempted defence of Barthian closedness by Kraemer looks less impressive. At least some approximate truths can occur in F_2, even given the "final" truth of F_1. Furthermore, it is in practice possible to point to parallels between religious ideas and behavior (the comparative study of religion is not, after all, a grand illusion). Such parallels may indeed have great significance in the dialogue and discussion between faiths and in the matter of criteria of truth.

It may then be concluded that the Barthian position runs into a peculiar difficulty if we conceive its being confronted by a similar position from within another faith. There would seem then no way to decide between the claims of F_1 and F_2. Barthianism can appear much more persuasive when the choice is not between faiths, but between faith and non-faith.

Nevertheless, the Barthian position surely points to an ineluctable aspect of religious discussion. For even if it might be possible in regard to some aspects of faith, the grounds upon which it is held, there has to be an irreduceable part which is taken on authority, or is simply given in revelation. There will be an analogous problem when different residues confront one another. But perhaps this conclusion is misconceived. Agreed, there may remain a simply "given" aspect of revelation, corresponding on the religious plane to the brute facts encountered in mundane experience. But there may still be criteria for determining the truth of revelation. That is, it is necessary to distinguish between the content of revelation and the criteria for determining its truth. It used, for instance, to be thought that Christ's miracles somehow guaranteed the authoritativeness of the Christian revelation.

As it happens, miracles do not serve very well here. First, as Hume pointed out, we have the strongest reason to reject belief in miracles, in that a miracle is something contrary to universal experience. It is easier to suppose that those who report or hand down stories of miracles are deceived or deceiving than that a law of nature, testified to by so much experience, has been broken. Second, a miracle is not just the breaking of a law of nature. It has to have some revelatory or religious significance. We already have to accept some religious presuppositions before we can understand that significance. Third, no one religion has a monopoly of miracle stories. And if anything, the direction of credibility runs in the opposite direction: it is not so much that because of miracles an authority is believed, but that because of authority miracles are believed. For instance, those who believe in a miraculous resurrection of Jesus do so, as often as not, because they already accept Christ as authoritative in his pre-resurrection teachings and activities.

Appeal to miracles is rather mechanical, in any case, and might even be thought to be a bit childish. It surely is a poor representation of the rather rich variety of reasons that are and could be appealed to in trying to show justification of the authoritativeness of a revelatory tradition. The grounds for faith in Christ or in the Buddha penetrate very much deeper than the mythic and miraculous occurrences surrounding their birth or whatever. It should, of course, interest us that miracles are handed down in the tradition. This fact is not irrelevant to the style of religious thinking. But it is not wise to pay overmuch attention to them. For it is easy to see that their role as supposed guarantees of truth is much inflated by a rationalistic and empiricist approach to religion. Rationalism and empiricism suppose that truth is to be derived from reasoning and mundane experience respectively; but clearly religious revelations and experiences do not belong to the approved sources of truth, and they cannot be derived from them. But miracles at least are observable events which do two jobs at once. They show that something strange is in dispute; and they provide observable evidence. They give this-worldly indications that there is something beyond the stereotyped representations of rational and empirical truth. In confronting these stereotypes on their home ground, so to say, they can somehow effect a guarantee of the beyond. But the substance of their power lies in the presupposition of those whom they influence that the sensible man does not, of his nature, take religion seriously until he is shocked into it. He begins by assuming that religion is irrational or cannot be established in experience; and then (hey presto) by a divine conjuring trick revelation of supernatural truths is guaranteed by strange events. In brief, the very appeal to the miraculous is itself a sign that the religious side of life is not taken with great seriousness. This parallels the position about language referred to in an earlier Chapter—that somehow religious language is in question, and so we have to begin from the literal everyday uses of terms and try to move on to their analogical uses in the context of religion. This forgot also that religion is already a viable part of human discourse and contains its own meaning.

I am not by this intending to argue that religion (or some particular religion) is therefore of necessity true. It is open to the sceptic to reject it all. I am only arguing that religion begins by having meaning (just as, for that matter, witchcraft does). Likewise, religious truth has its claims and its criteria. It is still open for the sceptic to think that none of the religions matches up to the tests; it is also open to him to think that the tests ultimately miss their point. But it is unnecessary to think that a criterion imposed by a prior scepticism about religion, and a rather crude failure to understand the richness of the tests of true faith, will much illuminate the discussion. In brief, the appeal to the miraculous (and its criticisms), especially in the eighteenth century, tend to miss the significance of religion.

I have referred to the richness and variety of reasons which might be appealed to in the justification of something as a revelation or authoritative source of true religion. Let us list a few of these reasons, both negative and positive. Negatively (and perhaps a little intellectualistically) "historical" faiths such as Christianity and Judaism need to be roughly right about the crucial historical facts. This is a reason why scientific-historical criticism of the Biblical material in the last century and a half or so has induced quite a furore. Christianity would surely be false unless certain historical facts were the case. If Jesus never lived, then how could there be any faith in the incarnate Christ? So if some facts do not hold, there would be a falsification of the faith—this is the reason for calling this historical criterion a negative one. For it could never be shown merely on historical grounds that the Christian faith is true. We might all accept that Jesus died by crucifixion under Pontius Pilate. But it would not follow from this that he died for men's sins, was a saviour, etc. The historical facts are necessary, but not sufficient, for the truth of the claims made about salvation, etc. So then the Judeo-Christian tradition needs to be roughly right about the historical facts. I say "roughly" since it is possible to retain faith in either Judaism or Christianity without believing all that is recorded by way of supposed history in the Old and New Testaments. (Indeed, supposing one had to retain it all as literal truth, one might have to reject faith, for there are many indications, from a purely historical point of view, of fallibility in the scriptures—a reason why there is sometimes a polarisation among those who contemplate them: on the one hand the literalist deductivists who strenuously claim the truth of every proposition contained in scripture, and on the other hand, the literalist agnostics who on scientific-historical grounds cannot swallow the whole lot and so reject the whole lot!)

Another necessary condition of acceptability of revelation is a mixture of the ethical and the historical. Still confining our examples to the Judeo-Christian tradition: suppose that tomorrow a new document were turned up in the sands of the Negev, which was seen to be an account of the life of Jesus (or Moses), but by usual historical criteria was much more reliable biographically than the Gospels (or the Old Testament). Suppose that is showed conclusively that Jesus wantonly murdered one or two people (or that Moses did). Would it then be easy to think of Jesus (or Moses) in the way in which the orthodox religious believers do? Would it still be possible to treat this real (not just technical) criminal as Son of God? There would be such a radical conflict between faith and conscience that the former would have to go. Although it is often claimed (and the claim cannot be shrugged off) that God challenges human values, there are breaking-points in reasonable faith. I cannot be asked to worship (say) a god who enjoins Nazi practices. (The breaking-point, alas, sometimes does not in fact occur: evil becomes identified with the highest good.)

Another negative criterion is inconsistency, though this is more formal than the preceding two criteria. It need not be an absolute self-contradiction (a topic discussed in the second Chapter). It can reveal itself as a rather intolerable tension between different elements of a faith. For example, we have already appealed to the mixed historical-ethical kind of criterion: something similar recurs when we contemplate the consequences of saying both that God is Creator and that he is perfectly good. For if he is Creator (certainly from the Christian point of view) he creates everything there is, and is not limited by the imperfection or irrationality of a preexistent material he may have to work with. (In short, the Christian doctrine is about creation *ex nihilo*, out of nothing: God is not like a sculptor having to work in stone, with all its difficulties and peculiarities.) But if all this is so, God is directly responsible for those features of the world which bring about suffering in men and animals. He may even be responsible for the tendencies in men and animals themselves to cause suffering to other men and animals. If so God is responsible for Dachau, and at least for earthquakes and pestilences. This seems to be in contradiction with his perfect goodness. What price his love? How much of a Father can such a one be? There is, in brief, a tension between two aspects of our faith in a good Creator. There are other cases of tension and even perhaps of contradiction in religious beliefs. They constitute prima facie a reason for rejecting faith.

The above negative criteria are not meant to be an exhaustive list; only a sample. It is time to turn to some positive criteria—those that tend to establish the truth of a faith, rather than its falsity. Let us begin with a thought drawn from Buddhism. The Buddha's teaching, it is claimed, is *ehipassiko*, a "come and see" matter. It can then be tested in experience, though the path is often long and difficult. Although the Buddha's insight is thought to go beyond that attainable by others, yet the adept can hope to gain a rather similar illumination. He will then "existentially" see the truth of the teaching and the rightness of the path. Somewhat similar remarks are sometimes made in the Christian context: those who commit themselves to Christ will come to see that he is the Truth—their faith will thus be justified in experience. Now it is doubtful whether such appeals to experience can be considered proofs; but they are clearly relevant to the truth and worth of a faith. It also is clear that such confirmations of truth start already from the given. The Buddha's teaching and the revelation in Christ are already given as something authoritative and promising. Within these limitations it is reasonable, though, to count experience as a criterion.

We need, though, to explore what is meant by 'experience' here. Often the Christian may be thinking that mysteriously and joyfully yet also sacrificially life "works out for him" after commitment to Christ, while before it was a mess. Such an appeal to 'experience' contains implicitly an appeal to fruits: "By their fruits ye shall know them," or more particularly, "By my fruits I shall know Him." One should therefore add the criterion of moral fruitfulness as conducing to confirmation. But it should be noted that judgments can be very complex. For fruits are clearly evaluated by reference to certain ideals and values (such as serenity and zeal) which themselves may derive their centrality from the shape of the religious tradition in question. The Buddhist may estimate fruits rather differently from a Christian, a Muslim from a Hindu. This does not make the appeal quite circular, for two reasons: first a religion needs to show that it at least has the power to produce the fruits that it values; and second, the fruits tie in with moral insights which men may have independently of commitment to a particular tradition.

But "experience," as well as meaning the lessons learned in living along a particular path, can also and more dramatically refer to experiences of conversion, insight, vision, and so on (such as the theophany in the *Gita* referred to earlier, and the conversion of Paul). These are thought somehow to reveal the beyond, the religious ultimate, and so enter into the fabric of reasons a man may give for his faith. Here again judgments become complex. There are many 'prophets' and others who can claim intuitive, ecstatic knowledge. Though these prima facie legitimate their teachings, they must also pass under scrutiny, and there need to be tests of genuine and false prophecy (a problem Paul faced in the early Church, just as in medieval times there was the question of who were and who were not genuine mystics who had an inner vision of the Godhead). Also, the degree of weight put upon such experiences can vary from community to community. Where people are expected to undergo conversion in some rather dramatic sense, religious experiences are then looked on not merely as sources of confidence in the truth of the faith as preached, but also as tests of whether the individual should count as having faith. This points to another variable.

Since revelation seems to be a relational concept (God reveals himself *to* someone), there is variation in the possible subjects to whom God reveals himself. It can be the individual and/or the community, or mankind at large. Emphasis on the communal aspect will tend to shift concern away from the experiences of all the faithful to the visions and insights of the saints and doctors of the Church; on the other hand, where the individual subject is empha- sised, one is more likely to get a demand for individual experience as a test of faith. However, these are more directly tests of faith than of the truth of revelation. But the two are connected, for a criterion is needed for discriminating who or what counts as the genuine tradi- tion, and it is that tradition that claims to mediate and embody the manifestations of the religious ultimate. Thus by consequence men often turn away from religion because of disillusion with the sacred institution or with the holy people who are supposed to maintain and exemplify the power of revelation.

This, it may be noted, is relevant to the problem of Barthian closedness discussed earlier. Even given a rigid and exclusive claim about revelation, there must be some test of who has faith and who does not. It is true that men may err, the criteria may not be over-precise and it is unwise to take the divine judgment into human hands. Yet the testimony that there is such a thing as saving knowledge of God becomes empty unless one can point to some of those who possess it. Suppose for the sake of argument the test has to do with the experience of conversion (and the signs in behavior that it is not falsely claimed). Then it becomes in principle possible to begin to compare such conversions with those of other traditions. (If someone in another tradition has a very similar experience with similar living fruits, it becomes difficult to stick to the view that there is only one way to the saving knowledge of God.) Let us consider here an oversimplified example.

Suppose there is a man brought up in the Christian tradition who yet drifts away from any Church allegiance, yet retaining an inner belief in Christ, though often hesitant. He becomes interested in the contemplative life, reading much in the Spanish mystics. He begins to put this interest into practice. He somehow, he knows not how, attains an experience of a dazzling obscurity which he conceives as giving him a perception of the religious ultimate. This resolves his hesitancies. He now claims to know that faith in Christ is the way to Truth, for was it not in the context of belief in Christ that he came to this contemplative experience? But now, let us suppose, he meets a Hindu holy man, who seems genuine, profound, sincere (and actually holy, unlike a number of holy men). The Hindu describes to him his own deep experience of a dazzling experience which gave him the realisation of his essential identity with Brahman, ultimate reality. But no mention of Christ. It then becomes a question as to whether the Hindu too has attained to the Truth. What does our Christian say? He could say one of two things. One is that they both somehow perceived the same Truth, and so it would be better to say that faith in Christ is *a* way, not the only way, to the Truth. Or he could say that the Hindu failed to attain the Truth for he did not have his inner vision in the context of faith in Christ. (A variation on the latter would be to say that the Hindu only had a partial view of the Truth.) The latter judgment is a little artificial, given the example as we have stated it, i.e., if the *only* difference between the Christian and the Hindu is that the Christian believes in Christ (though without connecting Christ up in a living way to Church sacraments, teaching, etc.). It would only begin to look plausible if the extra provided by the belief in Christ made a pervasive difference to the spirit of his search. In brief, it is not impossible to go on maintaining an essential difference between the two cases, but there is something of a struggle involved. This implies that like experiences should be treated alike, a way in which the appeal to experience functions in relation to religious truth-claims. Thus it looks impossible to shut off the closed circle entirely: for even on the most closed view there must be some manifested test of faith, and this inevitably enters into comparison with alternative paths.

Even so, we are still conceiving of the problem of what positive criteria could be used to validate *traditions*. It is not being suggested that one could derive or prove religious conclusions from religious experiences, etc. That is the appeal to them functions more as a "confirmation" of a preexisting system of revelation than as a premise from which such a system could be deduced. And therefore it is important to consider, sometimes at least, the origins of such systems: for in their origins another sort of "positive" criterion may lie. For instance, some religions trace their main origin to founders, prophets, etc. Thus it is not possible to treat of the question of the truth of the Christian faith or of Buddhism without estimating

Christ and the Buddha. "What think ye of Christ?" is not a rhetorical question; nor is it irrelevant that the Buddhist affirms that he "takes refuge in the Buddha." Likewise the Muslim recognises in the force, profundity, and beauty of the Koran that it was no false boast of Muhammad to have been the recipient of revelations from Allah.

Thus something must depend upon the estimate of the force and style of the founder or prophet of a religion, since he forms an important aspect of the focus of piety, and even in some cases of worship. Max Weber spoke of the charisma of such leaders. It is perhaps no guarantee of truth by itself that a founder is charismatic. (Hitler, alas, was charismatic.) But it draws attention to the manner in which the founder himself displays or manifests that which he also reveals. It is thus by no means irrelevant to appeal not just to the authority of (say) Christ, but to the content of his biography as mediated in the tradition. (There is of course the further question of whether the tradition has been historically accurate in its transmission of the biography: sometimes this is a really vital issue, as in Christianity—for the doctrine of the Incarnation makes it hard for the faith to be satisfied with an imaginary Christ, as though, if he had not been like that it would have been necessary to invent him like that, to paraphrase Voltaire.) In appealing to the force and style of life of the founders, etc., we are, of course, doing far more than looking at their moral characters. Though, as we saw, there might be negative moral bars to treating someone as divine, moral goodness is not enough. The kind of judgment made is somewhat similar to an aesthetic one. To say that the Buddha was serene, profound, spiritually penetrating; or that Jesus was challenging, delightful, authoritative, tragic—to say such things is not just to reflect upon the virtues of the people in question. It is to think of them as having a special mystery and force, a special right to command or attract loyalty, etc.

But should we think of humans in this way? Why pay attention to this sort of charisma? The only reply is that we are here considering religious claims in the concrete, not in the abstract. And we are looking at the considerations which are liable to move people. We have first to understand the criteria of truth. Then in a mood of criticism, perhaps disillusion, we may be in a position to wish all this away as another form of human folly. But religion depends on its givenness (in one terminology, its being revealed) and an important aspect of this givenness is the force of those who are at the center of the giving, for they constitute indeed part of the object which is presented for religious loyalty.

Behind the appeal to the charismatic force of founders can lie other considerations. A brief description of these can illustrate the force of suggestion, natural adjuncts, or that form of relationship between different parts of a religious system than that of entailment, to which I referred earlier.

Consider the Christian faith in Christ. It is not just that Christ was a teacher (though he was that). More importantly he is regarded as someone who acted in a certain way and thus saved mankind. His actions involved his death, and the sign of his victory over death and sin was (it is believed) his resurrection. What he did (and what was, so to say, done for him) was more important than the teachings, important as these may be for the Christian. But in order to understand these actions, it is necessary for the Christian to look back on prior Jewish history. The Christian sees Christ as a kind of fulfilment of the relationship between God and Israel disclosed in the Old Testament. But this relationship is set out in historical terms. Thus Christ appears at a certain point in a historical process, and in some vital way the ongoing historical process is relevant to the whole business of salvation. This is the chief reason why Christianity is dubbed an "historical" religion. But it may not strike everyone that history is as important as all this. Why should God thus reveal himself in history? Why should he not have a more timeless and universal impact on the world of men? These questions are by no means academic. They lie behind the reasons why Gandhi could not despite his sympathy for the Christian faith become a Christian. They lie behind the unease which many feel for the particularity of the Christian revelation, its essential scandal in pinning God's work so heavily down to a particular time and place and cultural milieu. They lie too behind the stirring doubts that we may feel in contemplating this particularity on the wider backcloth of the cosmos, given that there may be rational life not unlike ours scattered here and there through the teeming galaxies that stretch out vastly beyond our little center (and yet not center) of the universe.

In brief, the attempt to treat Jesus as the incarnate Lord, beginning from the question of his impact on us as mediated through tradition, itself is assisted by a prior conception—that God acts through history. Yet the traditional mythology of many peoples does not look on mankind's past in terms of a line or lines of events. The idea of a linear history is not the only picture; nor the valuation of the historical the only judgment that can be made. Traditional Indian cosmology conceives, for instance, of an infinite or virtually infinite succession of recurring phases of expansion and collapse of the cosmos—the endless repetition of stages of history, the relative insignificance of our epoch in the total rhythm of natural life. This very different picture militates against the simple acceptance of the question, "What think ye of Christ?" The background (and not merely the cultural background, but the general background of cosmology and value-judgments) is missing.

Yet there is a certain solidarity in the Christian picture, which can be expounded as follows to illustrate the "suggestive" connections between different aspects of a religious system and of religious experience. If we look at the accounts of the Creation in *Genesis* we notice two facts of general importance. First, the Creation merges imperceptibly into the history of mankind and of Israel in particular. There is a continuity between Creation and the Covenant. The Creation itself is presented in quasi-historical terms. The myth is adapted to the later chronicles. Of course we cannot be too literal in thinking of the Creation as being an historical event (though there have been many who have tried to take this literalistic path, and so to calculate the date at 4004 B.C.—but it is interesting that this attempt has been made, for it testifies to the appearance of continuity above mentioned: it also testifies, perhaps, to a kind of religious insecurity which projects the inner need for assurance outwards on to an unquestioning acceptance of scriptural propositions; but that is a debatable judgment). So then there is a suggestion built into the Creation narratives that points towards an evaluation of the importance of the historical process. Second, we may note that the orthodox interpretation of the narratives has insisted strongly on the idea that God creates out of nothing. This is another way of stressing the dependence of the world on God, even to the extent that the decision to create is seen as rather arbitrary—we thus depend upon a *fiat*. This is one mythic means of expressing the immense power of God in comparison with us and our environment, which lie at the bottom end of the polarity between holiness and unholiness, power and weakness, etc. Hence the narratives display in mythic form a very strong sense of the numinous experience of the Holy (also in general a monotheistic picture, which emerges in the course of the history of Israelite religion stresses the supremacy of the Holy, while polytheism tends to fragment and tame the different facets of religious experience). So, secondly, the Creation narratives testify to the Otherness of the divine Being, and our dependence upon him.

The one facet of the narratives has some solidarity, then, with the Christian account of salvation through historical acts. The second facet presents the problem of salvation. Human unholiness—man's distance from God—is partly realised through the responsibilities of action: the very distance leaves men elbow-room, so to say, while the cosmos as God's creation is good in principle and a worthy sphere of human action. Yet on the monotheistic principle only God can save, while there is a responsibility on the part of man for his own unholiness. How can he expiate his sin? How can he reach up to communion with the Holy One? Only if God condescends; or even descends. If God be both God and man he can simultaneously expiate human sin and grant salvation. Such is the logic lying behind traditional accounts of Christ's actions. We have, of course, treated the constellation of mythic and doctrinal ideas in a superficial way, and their surface meanings may not be acceptable to those who do not see man as a corporate being in some sense as well as a flock of individuals. But enough has been said, I hope, to bring out the way in which the different elements in the scheme suggest one another, and how there is a congruence between the Creation narratives and the story of redemption.

There is, then, a kind of aesthetic coherence within a religious system, which is the converse of the tensions which we referred to in the short list of negative criteria. The seeing of this solidarity, this organic nature, of the ideas and practices is itself relevant to estimating its truth. It is a way in which a religious scheme can make sense, and has its analogue in the beauty and coherence of some scientific theories. This is not of course to say that a religious scheme is a sort of theory. But it is an assemblage of given parts, these being drawn from diverse sources—sometimes from historical events (or memories thereof), sometimes forms of religious experience, sometimes aspects of the rites which reexpress such experiences, sometimes myth and symbolism lying to hand in the cultural environment of a growing religious tradition. The illumination which the parts offer one another, the coherence and sense of the assembled whole—these help to explain the acceptability or otherwise of a given scheme.

This picture of religious schemes of ideas is not intended to mean that religions are artificial creations, a kind of improvisation on themes lying to hand, like a collage. A religion may or may not be such. But it must remain an open question as to whether it is genuinely revelatory, and on one interpretation of "artificial" it could not be: it would be, so to say, a human invention, perhaps often motivated unconsciously. I do not want to imply by the above picture that a scheme cannot delineate properly and rather truly the religious ultimate. But it seems a realistic account of how things are. The different mythic and other elements woven into a scheme can sometimes be traced to particular cultural sources. But it is always open to the adherent of a faith to see these as symbolic materials which have been used in the communication of the truth from "beyond" to men. There is no reason why people should not express religious truth through mythic symbols lying to hand, just as religious truth can be expressed in a particular language (Sanskrit or Hebrew) lying to hand.

It was argued in the preceding Chapter, on the meaning of life, that limiting questions can find a kind of answer in religion. If this is so, then the effectiveness of a faith in providing deep and (in the required sense) meaningful accounts of the boundary situations of life will be an added criterion of its acceptability and truth. As with the aesthetic criterion, there is much vagueness here as to what counts as profundity and meaningfulness. But it is not to be supposed that all questions of truth depend upon equally clear criteria. It is the mark of an educated man, as Aristotle observed, to expect that degree of precision which the subject-matter allows. It will be no surprise that the rather poetic and mysterious qualities of religion should imply rather intuitive and inexact modes of estimating its truth and worth. We therefore forgive that kind of religious scholasticism which breaks down the mythic and the doctrinal into a series of clear distinctions only on condition (and this is a condition often satisfied) that it occurs in the context of a living and more diffuse faith. The older style Roman Catholic text-books, for instance, happily bore rather little relation to the living fabric of daily faith and practice; just as the over-precise lists of possible offences against monastic rules to be found in the Buddhist canon bear little relation to the actual meaning of the life of the *bhiksu* (monk).

The "positive" criteria that we have so far discussed need qualification. It follows from the earlier analysis of the problems of understanding religion and religious concepts that one cannot simply apply the criteria "externally." That is, it is necessary to enter into the form of life which claims some truth, by sympathetic imagination (or more strongly by commitment). It is not possible to discover the point of what is being asserted from a merely "external" point of view. These things being so, the most natural form of discussion about truth is through dialogue. That implies that F_1 does not pronounce on F_2 merely externally, but that its adherents enter into discussion and understanding with adherents of F_2. Such dialogue need not involve that over-enthusiasm for understanding which thinks that there must be agreement before there can be sympathy and intelligibility. (Do we not often value friends precisely because they do not think as we do?) It has sometimes been pointed out that there can be no dialogue without differences. If I do not hold to my own position, how can I enter into dialogue with another? If I already accept his position, there is nothing further to discuss. So by "dialogue" is meant the interplay of recognisably different positions, but with both parties trying to enter with sympathetic imagination into the values and claims of each other. What is not understood, in the relevant sense, cannot properly be discussed.

The list of positive criteria needs qualification in another way. There is no claim to completeness. The richness of positive criteria far outreaches the examples which have been given. Moreover, I have said nothing about the relation between religious and scientific claims (this is an issue to be reserved till later). Nor have I attempted to bring out more than cursorily the way in which questions of truth often concern the content of a particular faith rather intimately. That is, it is necessary to apply criteria of truth in the knowledge that some are more important for one faith than for another. For instance, the questions about the historical Jesus, which are bound to arise as a result of the application of the scientific-historical method to the scriptures will have a greater impact on Christianity (and for that matter Judaism) than upon Buddhism, which is less interested in its roots, more concerned with its fruits.

Behind all this, it is necessary that different faiths should make plain, so far as this is possible, the nature of the religious ultimate towards which they tend. For it would be ironic if different systems were to quarrel over the nature of ultimate reality when all the while they represented different approaches to the one goal. It is not altogether easy here to lay down criteria. As we have seen the conception of the religious ultimate tends to transcend the manifestations through which people have faith. But a sample of the problems here can be garnered from a passage in Wilfred Cantwell Smith's *The Meaning and End of Religion.*[7] The author is hostile to systems and thinks that religious divisions reflect an unnecessary concentration on doctrinal and other modes of differentiating one expression of truth from another. In the final resort, he does not believe in religions. He does not believe in Christianity, but he believes in true Christians. He prefers adjectives to nouns. In a later book, *Questions of Religious Truth*[8] he makes this point very explicit. In the earlier book he writes:

> The end of religion, in the classical sense of its purpose and goal, that to which it points and may lead, is God. Contrariwise, God is the end of religion also in the sense that once He appears vividly before us, in His depth and love and unrelenting truth all else dissolves; or at least the religious paraphernalia drop back into their due and mundane place, and the concept 'religion' is brought to an end.[9]

In the later work, there is something in rather similar vein:

> I still hold, then, that there are no nouns. Religious life begins in the fact of God: a fact that includes His intitiative, His agony, His love for us all without exception . . . Given that fact—and it is given; absolutely, and quite independently of whether or how we human beings recognise it; given that irremovable fact, religious life then consists in the *quality* of our response.[10]

Professor Cantwell Smith, in these quotations, seems to lay down in advance the proper description of the religious ultimate. He can scarcely succeed in persuading the Buddhist reader of the truth of what he says, for the Buddhist is not concerned to describe the religious ultimate in terms of God (and in general, the terms favored by Smith). But the latter is a sincere and learned person. What do we say about his proposal? How can it be generally admitted that God is the goal of all religion?

Despite the importance of trying to dig down behind the forms of religion, including both ideas and practices, it is also necessary to be clear that a certain form of description of the goal of religion (the true nature, the essence, the genuine object of worship, the aim of true contemplation, etc., etc.) may fail in dialogue. That is, it may prejudge the issue. It is hard for religious people, when confronted by other traditions, to fail to apply their own categories to them; though by the same token the compliment is returned. Thus it is necessary to see the religious ultimate, at least in the first instance, under the various sets of concepts and practices that serve both to define it and to point the way toward it. It is no use proposing a unity of religious goal in terms that are not universally or generally agreed (a fault, perhaps, in modern exponents of Hinduism, where the common assumption is that all religions are saying the same thing in the last resort: this can be a welcome change from rather ignorant judgments in the opposite direction—claims to uniqueness in certain respects when the facts of the comparative study of religion do not bear them out).

The need to see the religious ultimate under the guise of the conceptual schemes and religious practices which define them draws our attention to a feature of the logical situation. The complexity and organic nature of religious systems means that they severally gain an advantage and a disadvantage. The advantage is that the faith in question is determinate, and so has a claim to a stake in the world. The disadvantage is that it is liable to give a complex account of what it really thinks of as ultimately simple. In theistic terms: the description is highly elaborated, what with the history (for example) of Israel and God's dealings with it; yet in his own essence God is not, so to say, the collage that the doctrinal scheme is.

Perhaps there is an analogy with a theoretical concept in physics. For instance, the term *electron* is not intelligible in isolation: it gains its meaning through the complex of theory which describes and explains the micro-structure of the world. In being thus ramified, the concept itself is a complex one. But what it describes need not have the same complexity. Words are not pictures, where there is a literal resemblance between what is represented and what represents it: here certainly the complexity of what represents it is going to be reflected in the object represented, and conversely. Still, it may be answered, it is not quite correct to look on doctrinal schemes as composed of words; or rather, they in part refer to manifestations of the religious ultimate (say in history). The manifestation is complex—so there must be some complexity in the underlying Object. It was already argued in an earlier Chapter that the manifestations of God in salvation-history, of God in Christ, and of the Holy Spirit are the ground for the complex delineation of God's nature contained in the Trinity doctrine. Something seems to turn on whether we regard revelation as given in words or in manifestations (an issue akin to that as between deductivism and inductivism regarding the scriptures, referred to earlier).

It seems that revelation must contain both aspects. That is, the manifestations of the religious ultimate need to be interpreted in a certain way to be seen *as* manifestations of the ultimate. For instance, the career of Jesus is seen *as* manifesting the divine love in its activity of bringing redemption to men. But this aspect under which Jesus is seen requires words for its description. Thus revelation is a set of interpreted manifestations (and hence there is sometimes doubt about it from both directions—some supposed action of Christ hitherto seen as manifesting some aspect of the divine character may be subtracted by historical research; alternatively the action may be retained but the interpretation queried). What, then, is "given" in a religious tradition is a complex object—there are events, experiences, persons, etc., held to manifest the religious ultimate; there are mythic and symbolic interpretations of events, etc.; there are the doctrinal ideas which try to clarify the reference of these manifestations to the "beyond" and to show the interconnections and coherence between the different interpreted elements of the manifestations. This "given" focus of faith is seen through the community life and practices through which the ongoing tradition expresses itself. Preaching and religious teaching and living in a certain way are the modes by which the faithful can re-present this given focus.

I suggested earlier that the process of dialogue between faiths is the natural way for the exploration of questions of truth as between different religions. But it is also possible for a more total doubt to invade thought about religion. Can the criteria (other than the negative ones) move the agnostic humanist or the Marxist? Is there any way of trying to show that religion in general is a source of truth? Before turning briefly to this problem, it is worth looking at a query about the notion of dialogue.

The assumption of the discussion in this Chapter has been that religions present something for universal acceptance. This is however only true of some religions. Buddhism, Christianity, and Islam are, for instance, quite definitely missionary religions, which believe that the truth should be spread. Matters are more ambiguous in regard to Judaism and Hinduism, while ethnic religions tend to look upon themselves as the customary expression of life in a given community, not as something for export. There is a tension between the traditional, community aspect of religion and the notion of propositional truth. For truth is in an important sense, universal. It does not make sense to say that something is true for me but not for you (except in the sense that I believe p while you do not—but a comment on what people believe is not itself a comment on the truth of what they believe). There is a severe paradox in my saying: "There is a piano in the next room, but there is no need for you to believe what I have just said." In asserting something, I am telling you, trying to persuade you, asking you to believe something. If it is true that the earth goes round the sun, it is true no matter who you are. Central Americans are not exempt from believing it, just because ancient Aztec astronomy denied it, etc.

On the other hand, traditional customs do not need to be shared with others. There is no special call to homogenize human practices. Scotsmen can wear kilts if they want to; but that does not mean that Californians have to. This is a reason for the appeal of the thesis that all religions point to the same truth, for then it becomes possible to allow different customary practices to continue, but retaining a kind of ideological validity. The tension between the particularity of tradition and the universal requirements of truth tends to put ethnic religions at a disadvantage in their intercourse with missionary ones. (There are other cultural reasons for their being at a disadvantage, of course, and especially in the colonial era.) However, though it is wrong to see all religions as universalist, the notion of dialogue (which typically occurs between universalist faiths) is still useful; for questions of truth become relevant precisely when proposals of belief are being made, and this is clearly in a universalist situation.

Moreover, such a universalist situation arises when only one party to the dialogue is initially universalist. The other party needs himself to frame some universalist answer. Consider the following over-simplified discussion:

A: What I preach is for all men to believe.
B: But we B-people believe in the B-gods.
A: The A faith is immeasurably richer; look I will show you.
B: I can see it is a fine faith, but not for us B-people.
A: But what I preach, as I said, is for all men, including the B-people.
B: No; you can stick to your faith, we to ours.
A: But what about the truth: does that not concern you?
B: Yes, we must all believe in the great Spirit, but he manifests himself in different ways to different men. For us B-people the B-gods are right and enough. Other folk have other gods.

This over-simplified discussion represents a recurring theme in the interplay between missionary and non-missionary faiths.

Now we can turn to the larger question of the criteria of truth as between the religious position and agnostic humanism. It may be possible to cite a selection of positive criteria that may be relevant once one has made the assumption that truth can be found in one or other of its revealed, traditional manifestations. But the humanist is sceptical of this very point. There seems to be an impasse on every side. If I appeal to Paul's conversion as a reason for belief in the divinity and power of Christ, the answer is that we might be able to explain this event on purely psychological grounds. If one points to the charismatic nature of the Buddha, the answer is that this does not show that the Buddha has some kind of transcendental origin or destiny. If I point to the way the Israelites were led out of Egypt, the answer is that a natural series of events has later been given a mythic interpretation, which one does not need to accept. If I point to the living fruits of the faith in the work of many saints and heroes, the answer is that religion indeed is inspiring, but false beliefs can be quite as effective as true ones. If I point to the way in which religion brings healthy confidence in the boundary situations of life, the answer is that perhaps we have to reconcile ourselves to lack of confidence.

The situation could be put crudely by saying that the humanist retains the supposed manifestations of the religious ultimate, but does not accept them as manifestations of anything beyond themselves. The situation is rather an ironical one. Anything that *could* be appealed to by way of evidence is prevented from being evidence, for the presupposition that there is something unseen, transcendent, which is manifested in events and experiences, etc., is not accepted. At first sight, there seems to be a strong analogy between this situation and an aspect of the philosophical problem of other minds.

I cannot see into another person's consciousness, so to say. I can see him grimacing, smiling, talking; but if I am sceptical as to whether he has a conscious mind (the way I have one), how can I ever get rid of my scepticism? All the behavior he produces is of no avail, for it can be interpreted simply as evidence of itself and no more. Can I not construct a coherent picture of his activities by reducing them all to patterns of behavior? I can leave out the mind perfectly well. There seems to be an impasse. My scepticism forever precludes its own demise.

The analogy might lead us to think of the kind of humanism I have described as "philosophical humanism." It is to do with a general scepticism about the transcendent aspect of religious manifestations. It is to be distinguished from what may be called "substantive humanism," which is the rejection of religious beliefs for substantive and particular reasons—e.g., the problem of evil, the falsity of literalist claims about evolution, the dishonesty of some religious tradition, doubt about the possibility of knowing anything historically about Jesus, and so on. A rather violent expression of substantive humanism was the burning of churches and killing of priests that broke out in many parts of Spain at the start of the Civil War. Hugh Thomas in *The Spanish Civil War*, writes:

If they had disgraced the *métier*, and had, say, in the past never worn a clean collar for the funeral of a poor man, but always had done so for a rich man, they would be killed . . . The *social* motive for killing explains the springs of the religious onslaught. The Spanish working class attacked churchmen because they thought them hypocrites and because they seemed to give a false spiritual front to middle-class society or upper-class tyranny.[11]

The anti-religious outbreaks in Spain did not deny the possibility of faith in principle: but they rejected religion in practice.

Philosophical humanism would present an insoluble problem for the proponent of religion, unless it turned out that ordinary knowledge somehow implied the necessity of a transcendent being. This would provide the transcendental reference for the religious manifestations (rather after the style of the article by Ian M. Crombie,[12] discussed in Chapter II). Thus, one way out of the impasse would be to establish the validity of natural theology as traditionally understood: for this would supply proofs or arguments for the existence of a transcendent Being. (It would not, however, help with Buddhism, where a different set of arguments would be necessary, to show the actuality of a transcendent state of liberation.) The topic of the proofs will concern us in the next Chapter.

There might too be another way out of the impasse, from the standpoint of the defender of religion. Philosophical humanism reflects a situation where the issue between faith and its adversaries is no longer an experimental one. As John Wisdom pointed out in his famous article "Gods" reprinted in his *Philosophy and Psychoanalysis*, we have moved beyond the point where we could settle matters like Elijah on Mount Carmel, calling down fire on his altar in competition with the practitioners of another religion.[13] (It may not of course be that matters were ever *really* settled in that way.) So it seems that religious claims are neither verifiable nor falsifiable. But does this impugn their status as assertions? Wisdom tries to exhibit their status by means of a parable. Two people return to their long-neglected garden, to find some of the plants doing remarkably well, though there are lots of weeds too:

They examine the garden ever so carefully and sometimes they come on new things suggesting that a gardener comes and sometimes they come on new things suggesting the contrary and even that a malicious person has been at work. Besides examining the garden carefully they also study what happens to garden left without attention. Each learns all the other learns about this and about the garden. Consequently, when after all this one says "I still believe a gardener comes" while the other says "I don't" their different words now reflect no difference as to what they have found in the garden, no difference as to what they would find in the garden if they looked further and no difference about how fast untended gardens fall into disorder. At this stage, in this context, the gardener hypothesis has ceased to be experimental, the difference between one who accepts and one who rejects not now a matter of the one expecting something the other does not expect.[14]

It would look as if the two people just had different feelings towards the garden; but the parable indicates that there is more. Both parties accept the same facts, but one arranges them in a different way from the other: and indeed this arrangement leads one to assert a fact (or supposed fact) not asserted by the other, even though there is no experimental issue any more involved. The parable thus leads us beyond verifiability and falsifiability as criteria of what count as assertions. But also the parable is relevant to the problem of what we have called philosophical humanism. For here the issue between him and the exponent of religion is not so much a matter of experimental fact as a matter of the way in which each sees the manifestations of religion. For the one they are manifestations of the religious ultimate (etc.); for the other they are just psychological, sociological, and other sorts of phenomena.

It is true that the parable seems to be written from within the context of questions about the design and signs of providential order in the universe (and thus within the context of theism, especially as conceived by philosophers). But it has a more general application. Its force, perhaps, partly derives from the fact that this is the only world we know. Questions about how to interpret this single world are different from those concerning repeatable and experimental events. There is no multiplicity of universe whereby we can check up by repeated observation on their essential nature. We are faced with the question of interpreting a single world. From the point of view of the parable, this is perhaps the "natural" world—the environment of human beings, rather than the cosmos as including different dimensions of human feeling and experience; but whether that is a right interpretation or not, there is no reason why we should not include under the head of "the world" the supposed manifestations of the religious ultimate, such as the experience of the Holy. Should these be moved into the center of the picture? Or should they stay at the periphery? If they stay at the periphery they can be "explained away" in terms of the rest of the world; if they are at the center, the world itself is seen in the light that they shed. Thus the situation is analogous to that of the couple who come back to their untended garden. Taking up the position of philosophical humanism, we do not dispute the facts. What is disputed is the correct interpretation of them: which pattern seems to effect the best account of the way the whole is?

On this account, the issue in the dialogue between religion and humanism has to do with the weight that is put on the supposed manifestations of the religious ultimate. If little weight is put on them, they are relegated to peripheral phenomena which can be subsumed under others in the world; if much weight is put on them the process is reversed. But what could lead anyone who does not already do so to put much weight on them; and what could lead someone who already puts much weight on them to cease to?

A preliminary thought about this concerns the secret suspicion that some may feel at the demands made earlier in this book about the necessity of entering in to the meaning of religion, if only by the use of sympathetic imagination. This already implies taking religious values and claims *seriously*. Does this then not mean that the agnostic is required to move already in the direction of shifting religious manifestations more to the center of his world-picture? Is he not beginning to compromise his position by entering into religious meanings? Such a secret suspicion may account for the crassness of many outside criticisms of religion—there is a fear of sympathy, which threatens the agnostic belief (but conversely, there is much crassness in religious accounts of "outsiders," springing perhaps from an unconscious fear that understanding the motives of substantive and philosophical humanism threatens the dearly held beliefs of faith). But the taking of religious forms of life seriously need not be regarded as a threat. Or if it is a threat, that is too bad. How else could one hope to estimate their worth and truth? But in any case one can be sympathetic without being committed, and there is certainly no ultimate necessity to move religious claims into the center of one's world-picture just because they are taken seriously. They can be taken seriously and then be discarded, just as one can come to know a person well without making friends.

What would making friends be, however, in the religious context? What would it be for the humanist to begin moving religious manifestations into the center of his world-picture, allowing them thus to become the key to the pattern there discerned? (Conversely, how does one lose trust in them as the key?) It is hard to see how there can be any movement here which does not take the form of a sort of "beguiling" of the humanist by what he encounters in the manifestations of religion. For religious claims to move towards the center they must be more impressive, more illuminating. Their impressiveness in part depends on the grip which the appropriate sentiments begin to have, in part on the charismatic power of the focus of loyalty; the illumination has to do with the coherence of the object presented through the mythic, doctrinal, and ritual aspects of a tradition, and in part to do with the way in which it meets the limiting questions and boundary situations the humanist confronts. Since it is religion itself that has to beguile, the criteria of true religion mentioned earlier must come into play; religion has to be seen to make sense in its own terms (just as being beguiled by history means that I have to apply historical criteria in determining what is a piece of historical writing). Conversely, loss of belief could be not so much substantive (being persuaded by particular pieces of evidence contrary to the set of beliefs one holds, etc.), as due to the fading of beguilement. Typically, though, the two go hand in hand: for religion is not just a general thing, but takes the form of particular faiths, and these faiths can fade because, by the appropriate criteria, they no longer look very convincing.

It is perhaps rather irrational-seeming to lay stress on the impact of religion in beguiling people from a non-religious position to a religious one. To speak of such a charismatic force is it seems to concede that rational considerations do not weigh very much. To this there are two replies. First, reasons take their character from the subject-matter; to believe in religion for religious reasons is not irrational. Second, the situation of the philosophical humanist is on the other side of reasoning, in a sense: what could count as religious reasons are ruled out in advance, because the idea of the religious ultimate is denied, so that evidences can no longer be evidences in the intended direction. In this limiting case of humanism, what more can be said than if religion takes a grip, the humanist can move towards an interpretation of reality in religious terms? And conversely, where the presupposition is in favor of religious faith, beyond the evidences that might count for or against any particular form of it, what more can be said than that after all the holy might not seem any more of importance? It would become meaningless, in the sense of lacking in what we earlier called "living meaning."

This Chapter has attempted to show that it is necessary to take the idea of the "given" or revelation seriously. Religions present a certain range of objects, and the way they do this is complex, since there are doctrines, mythic interpretations of events, religious experience, the ongoing life of the community, etc. The usual theological models of revelation (as deductivist, inductivist, etc. in character) are useful perhaps, but they do not bring out the richness of the situation. Nor do simple appeals to scriptural revelation bring out the actual complexity and richness of the criteria of truth in religion, though we were only able to look at a rather short list of these criteria. (For a fuller discussion of inter-religious arguments, see my *A Dialogue of Religions*, reprinted as *World Religions: A Dialogue*.[15])

We have left on one side one way out of the impasse created by the confrontation of religion by philosophical humanism. Is it possible to begin from non-religious factors to establish religious conclusions? Is a natural theology possible? If we can argue from the world to God, then this would be a basis other than the charismatic force of the Object presented in a given religion for accepting in principle the notion of a transcendent Being who or which might have manifestations in the world of human experience. It happens that much philosophising about religion has turned on these arguments. If I have left their consideration so late, it is in the interests of presenting a more full-bodied picture of religious concepts in their actual habitat, rather than beginning with the abstractions that can gain too much attention. Religion is at least as much a matter of revelation and living manifestation as of metaphysical arguments. But to the latter we now can turn.

Notes

1. Ninian Smart, *Reasons and Faiths* (New York: Humanities, 1959).
2. William A. Christian, *Meaning and Truth in Religion* (Princeton: Princeton University Press, 1964).
3. Erich Fromm, *The Dogma of Christ* (New York: Holt, Rinehart and Winston, 1963).
4. Roy S. Lee, *Freud and Christianity*.
5. Hendrik Kraemer, *The Christian Message in a Non-Christian World* (Grand Rapids, Mich.: Kregel, 1961).
6. R. C. Coburn, "The Concept of God," *Religious Studies*, 2, 1, pp. 61 ff.; and Smart, *op. cit.*
7. Wilfred Cantwell Smith, *The Meaning and End of Religion* (New York: Macmillan, 1962).
8. Wilfred Cantwell Smith, *Questions of Religious Truth* (New York: Scribner), p. 122.
9. Smith, *The Meaning . . . , op. cit.*, p. 181.
10. Smith, *Questions . . . , op. cit.*, p. 123.
11. Hugh Thomas, *The Spanish Civil War* (New York: Harper & Row, 1961), p. 232.
12. Ian M. Crombie, in Antony Flew and Alasdair MacIntyre (eds.), *New Essays in Philosophical Theology* (New York: Macmillan).
13. John Wisdom, "Gods," in *Philosophy and Psychoanalysis*.
14. *Ibid.*, p. 149.
15. Ninian Smart, *World Religions: A Dialogue* (Baltimore: Penguin Books).

Chapter Five ❧

❧ ❧ ❧ On Religion and Nature

It is likely that any attempted proof of God's existence will not go the whole way to establishing the existence of God as conceived in the full religious context. This is because the delineation of God in the latter context involves a complex doctrinal scheme, which reflects the variety of manifestations of God in the tradition. So the God of natural theology must surely be thinner than the Object of worship. But though such a gap exists between the two, this is itself no argument against the project of trying to show God's existence by beginning from the natural universe. The objection simply amounts to saying that natural theology could not do the whole job of establishing the truth of a given religion. But it might do part of the job: it might give grounds for belief; and above all it might give credence to the idea that there is a transcendent religious ultimate which can be seen in its revealed manifestations more richly.

Quite a wide variety of arguments have been used to attempt to show the existence of God, not merely in the Western tradition, but also elsewhere. (An account of Indian arguments and counterarguments is contained in my *Doctrine and Argument in Indian Philosophy*.[1]) It is only possible here to attend to a few of the more important ones. Immanuel Kant reduced the forms of speculative arguments to three—the Ontological, the Cosmological, and the Teleological (or Argument from Design). Our attention will mainly be directed at the latter two, since we had occasion to discuss briefly in the previous Chapter the objections to the Ontological Argument. There are also attempts to argue to God from moral and religious experience, etc., but to some extent these will have been taken care of in our treatment of limiting questions in morals, and in the general discussions of the validity of religious experience both hitherto and later on (when we shall consider Freudian and other theories about the genesis of religion).

It is useful to approach the arguments through the treatment given by Aquinas. For Aquinas has an important part in the Roman Catholic tradition—so much so that most expositions from the Roman Catholic side of the possibility of a natural knowledge of God (i.e., one not relying upon revelation) are expressed in terms that go back to Aquinas. By the papal encyclical of Leo XIII in 1879, Roman Catholics are enjoined to treat the works of Aquinas with the greatest seriousness, and not to depart from the conclusions thereof except for very good reason. This in its way and in its circumstances was an enlightened pronouncement—it did much to revive Catholic learning. The only trouble has been that Aquinas has himself been treated by many Catholics almost as revelation: and this washes out the distinction between what men can know of God independently of acceptance of the given, traditional presentation of the supreme Object of Christianity and what they can know by reflection on the world. This is not the only instance where custom, tradition, and authority have tended to blur distinctions. Even so, the Aquinas tradition represents an important view of the possibility of knowledge of God: and Aquinas himself was a great philosopher and theologian, needless to say.

The first three arguments of the five (the "Five Ways," i.e., to the natural knowledge of God) propounded by Aquinas are usually regarded as different versions of the Cosmological Argument. The first, which like the others has its roots in the philosophy of Aristotle, is commonly described as the argument from motion. A better word would be "change," since the key concept had, in its Greek context, a wider sense than "motion" in English (or even perhaps the equivalent in Aquinas' medieval Latin). "Motion" has to do with being in one place now and another place thereafter. But this is only one instance of change in general. For instance, if I blush, there is a change of color in my cheeks. This is not a matter of my cheeks being in one place now and another place in a moment's time: it is rather a matter of my cheeks being sallow now and reddish in a moment's time. There is such a thing as change of quality as well as change of place. But (and now we embark on Aquinas' argument), every change from what a thing could be to what it is—from potentiality to actuality—is a result of something else. And this something else has to be actual not potential: it must not just have the capacity to be of such and such a quality or in such and such a place: it must actually be thus or there. Whatever is changed must be changed by something else in the appropriate state to change it. But there cannot be an infinite chain of changers. If so, the process would not get started. So there must be a first changer (or First Mover). And this is what everyone understands to be God.

The second way starts from the agent rather than from what is changed, but in essence repeats the same line of reasoning. Two steps are crucial: one is the notion that an infinite chain would not do, for then there would be no change or causation now. The other is the identification of the First Mover or First Cause with God.

The third way is a bit different. Things can either exist or not exist. This is obvious from the fact that they come into existence and pass away. (Thus, to use an example which Aquinas does not use, my pet rabbit once did not exist, even as a gleam in its father's eye; it will eventually die.) But let us suppose that at one time there was nothing in existence: then how could anything come to exist? For a thing can only come to exist if something else exists. So there would be nothing now. One must therefore suppose that there is a necessary being whose existence explains the existence of everything else. Such a necessary being would have to be such that it is not contingent: does not come into and out of existence because of other things.

I have stated this argument without including a complication in Aquinas' argument, to do with everlasting beings, which can, according to Aquinas, exist, and which therefore do not come into existence, etc. But he regards these as requiring explanation in terms of a properly necessary being, i.e., one containing the explanation of its existence in itself.

It does not take too much reflection to see that the three Ways outlined above depend upon the thesis that one cannot have an infinite chain of causes. But this is paradoxical. For elsewhere Aquinas argues that the universe might be everlasting—i.e., an infinite chain of causes and effects, etc.—were it not for the information supplied by revelation. Aquinas took *Genesis* to mean that the world was created a finite time ago. A major attempt to explain away this paradox—an attempt which is certainly in line with what Aquinas seems to have meant about everlasting beings, etc.—is to say that Aquinas is not so much concerned with "horizontal" causation as "vertical." It is not that he is arguing for a First Cause in time. It is not that he is somehow tracing causes backwards till we reach a first term in this sequence. Rather it is that here and now I depend on some other existing feature of the world. (My breathing, for instance, on the existence of air; the existence of air on the state of the planet; the state of the planet on some fundamental physical and biological laws; these in turn on the overall state of the cosmos—naturally I here give an "up-to-date" set of examples of what might be meant.) This vertical relation of dependence cannot be infinite, on this argument; though the horizontal, temporal one could be.

This is not very persuasive in one way; but it is highly suggestive in another. Putting the unpersuasiveness rather crudely: the argument says that state A at t_1 (a given time) depends on state B at t_1 and so on; or changing our language to things, thing A at t_1 depends on thing$_2$, and this on thing$_3$, . . . and so on. But there is no reason in principle why there should not be an infinite number of things, just as there is no reason in principle why the cosmos should not have existed for an infinitely long time (indeed some modern cosmologies postulate both infinity in time and in extent: the extent in turn implies infinity of galaxies, etc.). There is no more incoherence in the thing series than in the time series. The substitution therefore of a vertical order of causation for a horizontal one does not make the argument any more convincing. But it does suggest a way of transposing the argument into different language, where it would seem to have real force.

The language is the language of explanation. This too, to put matters crudely, proceeds both horizontally and vertically. If I ask for the explanation of why there is a rainbow now in the sky, I can be given a kind of historical answer which will show how the conjunction of sunshine and rain came to be present in this area. But at the same time I can be given an explanation that has to do with the properties of light, etc., under certain conditions. It happens that our various sets of vertical explanations are not fully unified: there remain separate sciences. Yet there remains the hope of an overall unified theory which will embrace what is now included under the various sciences. (Such a unification has already occurred as between physics and chemistry.) In principle, then, we look for the possibility of deducing the variety of phenomena in the universe from a few fundamental features thereof. But then we can still go on asking why these fundamental features exist. But there must be a stopping place somewhere, for any vertical explanation of the few fundamental features would refer to some even more fundamental features. But if the business of explanation is to work at all, we have to put up with some "brute" first principles. Yet *still* we may go on asking. This is like the case of the limiting questions discussed in an earlier Chapter.

This seems to reveal a twin demand lying at the end of scientific explanations: the demand first for a further explanation, and the necessity, second, that this should not itself be a scientific explanation. The dependence of the world on a transcendent Being seems to satisfy both these requirements, provided the idea of the transcendent is filled out to make the claim escape emptiness. For example, it does not do any good to say: "And the reason for these 'brute' features of the universe is because there is an X which accounts for them." (This would be like saying, "The reason why bamboo grows so tall is that something causes it to grow so tall.")

We could approach the argument in another way which links up, though not very directly, with Aquinas' Third Way, with its idea of a necessary being whose necessity is not derivative. The argument and its analogues have been criticised by philosophers persuaded of the invalidity of the Ontological Argument on the ground that it contains the Ontological Argument. Does not the idea of a necessary being imply that its existence can be deduced from its essence?—and is not this the nerve of the Ontological Argument? Let us for the moment interpret the Third Way in this sense. What is suggestive about it then is perhaps not the notion of a necessary being, but rather the notion that other things are contingent. Perhaps the argument could be revamped by putting it thus: If we contemplate the cosmos, we soon realize that its existence is contingent—it is conceivable that it might not have existed. But about anything that might not have existed it is reasonable to ask for an explanation of why it does. In this case, the entity which explains the existence of the cosmos must lie "beyond" it—must be a transcendent Being.

It should be noted in this case too that we have reached the boundary of scientific explanation. The latter, as we saw, has to do with relating one feature or state of affairs of the cosmos to some other. It operates, so to say, "internally" to the cosmos. To ask for an explanation of the cosmos itself, as a whole, is necessarily to go beyond the bounds of scientific reasoning.

But the argument, even in this revamped form, seems to have an Achilles' heel. If we can ask why the cosmos exists, on the ground that it is conceivable or logically possible that it might not have, we can ask precisely the same question about God (or whatever it is that is supposed transcendently to explain the existence of the cosmos). Here is a dilemma. Either God's existence has to be made necessary, so he can be the long-stop of explanations; but in that case *God* becomes a self-contradictory notion (as according to the argument of Findlay's "disproof"): or God's existence is contingent, and he too requires explanation. There is a further trouble. Even suppose that we allow the idea of a necessarily existing thing, why should the cosmos not be it?

It looks as though there is a certain arbitrariness at where we stop. If God's existence in turn has to be explained, why not stop at the cosmos? We must begin with a brute fact somewhere. Perhaps the only argument left in favor of going beyond the cosmos to the transcendent is as follows.

At least trying to give an answer to the question of why the cosmos exists represents an advance; it is going an important stage further along the vertical line of explanations. The existence of the cosmos poses a problem. The idea of Creation gives some kind of answer, even if it poses its own problem. But as we have seen, to function as such an advance the explanation in terms of a transcendent Being must be filled out, given some content. It is a curious fact about Aquinas' arguments that they should conclude (having established the existence of a First Cause, Necessary Being, etc.): "This all men speak of as God," ". . . and this everyone understands to be God," ". . . to which everyone gives the name of God." For what in fact people mean by God is a good deal richer than the notion of a First Cause. If we seriously use the concept of God we are going beyond what the conclusions actually warrant. It is as if I have produced evidence to someone that there is a very influential man in Rome, and he jumps to the further conclusion that I mean the Pope.

But then there is no reason, if we pose the problem in terms of explanation, why the so-called "conclusion" should be capable of being deduced from the "premises." On the contrary, the direction of implication should be the other way round. For example, if the problem is to explain why eclipses of the moon occur, it is necessary to have some theory about the solar system, and this cannot be deduced from the fact that eclipses occur; but on the contrary, the eclipses can be deduced from the theory. The fact that the theory fits well means that the occurrence of eclipses is some sort of confirmation of the theory (in particular, if they occur at the intervals predicted by the theory, etc.); but they do not entail the theory. So there is no reason in principle why the so-called "conclusion" of the argument from the contingency of the cosmos should be capable of being deduced from the premiss. It is quite respectable to go beyond the evidence!

But that means that there is no guarantee that one particular transcendent-type explanation is the true one. Suppose, for the sake of argument, we fill out our explanation in a religious way. We see the problem of the contingency of the cosmos as partially solved by the Christian doctrine of Creation. It still remains possible that some other religious explanation can be advanced, for instance one framed in Vedantin terms. Thus the problem of the contingency of the cosmos does not by itself point unambiguously at a theistic explanation. Yet this is only to recognise what is implicit in the idea of natural theology anyway, that for a "full" knowledge of God one must go beyond reasoning to revelation; and there are of course alternative (supposed) revelations. It is impossible to escape the question of the criteria of revealed truth, which we discussed in the previous Chapter.

To sum up so far. It looks as if the best that can be done for the Cosmological Argument is to treat it not so much as a proof as the expounding of a problem. The easiest way to do this is by the use of the concept of explanation; here we reach a boundary situation, beyond the point where any further scientific explanations can be given (for they involve relating different features of the cosmos together, while the question now is about the existence of the cosmos as a whole). For a transcendent-type explanation to be effective, it has to be given content. One possibility is to give it a religious content. Then we reach a point where what is being said is that (say), the Christian doctrine of Creation gives an explanation of the existence of the cosmos. But other possibilities are open. Moreover, it is still open to someone to accept the brute existence of the cosmos. (He would have to accept the brute existence of God, if he did go beyond the cosmos, anyway.) Would there be criteria for choosing between the various possibilities?

First, there would be the criteria sampled in the previous Chapter. But supposing one accepts (say) the Christian revelation already, partly on the basis of these criteria, what good does the Cosmological Argument do? Conversely, if religion is rejected, surely such a problematic line of reasoning is not going to tip the scales. Still, the Cosmological Argument does seem to do *something* extra. It constitutes a ground (even if a tentative one) for linking up the contingency of the world with what is given in the theistic tradition. It is thus a ground for that shifting of the manifestations and values of religion into the center of one's scheme of thinking about the world which we described in the previous Chapter.

But it nevertheless relies on a very bare piece of "evidence"—the existence of the cosmos. The argument would retain what force it has whatever the world were like. The cosmological problem would exist as much in hell as in paradise. There would be something of a paradox reflecting, between bouts of pain in hell, that the very existence of such a world gives one ground for seeking a transcendental explanation of it, possibly in terms of divine Creation. It therefore appears as if the theistic solution to the cosmological problem must gain its plausibility from some signs, in the actual constitution of the cosmos, of the holiness and goodness of the Creator. The Cosmological Argument, then, by no means can stand on its own legs. It must make use of two crutches. On the one hand, there must be something given from the side of religion, so that the concept of a transcendent Being is filled out and given body. On the other hand, the divinity of the Creation must be reflected somehow in the natural world.

A point rather similar to this one was made in the Eighteenth Century, though in a rather different context of discussion, by Bishop Butler, who attempted to show that the constitution of the world is analogous to and of a piece with revealed religion. This creates the presumption that they both proceed from the same source. (These ideas are worked out in his *Analogy of Religion*, extracts from which are reproduced in my *Historical Selections in the Philosophy of Religion*.[2]) A possible way of discovering such an analogy to revealed religion in the natural world is through the third of the major arguments for God's existence—the Teleological Argument or Argument from Design. A version of this constitutes Aquinas' Fifth Way. Before moving to it, however, let us glance briefly at his Fourth Way.

This is taken from the gradation to be found in things, which are said to be more or less good, true, noble, etc. But the relative goodness, etc., of a thing depends on the degree to which it approximates to the maximum. Gradation therefore implies the existence of a maximum (the most good, the truest, the noblest). But further, the maximum in any given category is the cause of everything falling under the category: e.g., fire, being the maximum of heat, is the cause of all hot things. So there must be a supremely perfect Being which is the cause of being, goodness, etc., found in things. "And this we call God."

This argument is not very convincing. There are at least three objections that can be brought against it. The first is that it is not very realistic to think that the use of expressions like "better" and "worse," "nobler" and "less noble," implies the existence of a maximum to which these gradations are referred, for two reasons. One is that it is sufficient to make comparisons between given instances of goodness, etc. For instance, I can tell that A is a better baseball player than B, by various criteria (e.g., his batting average is higher), and without thinking that there is a supremely good baseballer whom they both fall short of. Again, even if we did refer such estimates to an ideal specimen (I might have in mind the specifications of an ideal peach, for instance, even though I had never encountered one), there is no need for this ideal specimen to exist. The second main objection is that it is doubtful, to say the least, to think that the maximum in a given genus is the cause of the other things falling under it. Aquinas' example, about fire, is hardly convincing. What we ordinarily call fire is not, of course, the hottest heat-phenomenon to be encountered, as a matter of fact: the middle of an H-bomb is much hotter than a burning log. In what sense is the middle of an exploding H-bomb the cause of my fire at home? The best that can be said is that a unified theory of heat can be evolved, but the causes of heat then become complex, to do with friction, the behavior of particles, etc. Aquinas' argument belongs to the era of a picture of science which has since been transcended. The third main objection is that the same form of argument ought to establish the existence of something maximally evil. The traditional reply to this objection is that evil is not something positive—it is the absence of a perfection. The worse in brief is equivalent to the less good, and so occurs low down on the scale running up to the maximum. However, it does not seem realistic to treat all cases of badness in this way. Admittedly, a thing is often bad because it lacks something good: a curry may be poor because certain vital spices have been left out. But a person who is cruel is not just someone who lacks kindly dispositions (one can lack these without being cruel); rather it is someone who takes an active delight in torturing others, etc. Again, pain is not just absence of proper functioning of the organism (though the lack of proper functioning may indeed cause pain); it is itself a positive sensation.

These last remarks are, incidentally, relevant to the attempt to solve the problem of evil by seeing evil not as something positive but rather as the lack or privation of goodness. If the objection made above to the Fourth Way is valid, it works too against this mode of dealing with the problem of evil. There is a clear discussion of this point in Frederick R. Tennant's *Philosophical Theology*, reprinted in my *Historical Selections in the Philosophy of Religion*.[3]

The problem of evil is also relevant to the project of discerning signs of divine Creativity in the natural world. For it can be argued that even if there were found such signs, the existence of evil would constitute signs running in the opposite direction. One way in which this situation might be regarded is outlined in Basil Mitchell's contribution, in *New Essays in Philosophical Theology*, to the discussion about falsification and meaninglessness.⁴ For Mitchell (I would think rightly) it is not possible to evade the problem of evil by thinking of God's love as quite different in kind from human love, so that the existence of evil does not stand in the way of ascribing love to God: then indeed the notion of divine love is evacuated of meaning. Rather, evil *does* constitute counter-evidence to God's goodness. But it is possible (Mitchell writes a parable to illustrate the point) to hold a belief for which there is both pro-evidence and counter-evidence. Such beliefs, he affirms, can be treated

> in at least three different ways: (1) as provisional hypotheses to be discarded if experience tells against them; (2) as significant articles of faith; (3) as vacuous formulae (expressing, perhaps, a desire for reassurance) to which experience makes no difference and which make no difference to experience. The Christian, once he has committed himself, is precluded by his faith from taking up the first attitude: "Thou shalt not tempt the Lord thy God." He is in constant danger, as Flew has observed, of slipping into the third. But he need not; and, if he does, it is a failure in faith as well as in logic.⁵

But for the parable to work, there must be pro-evidence. It *could* be that all this derives, so to say, from revelation, though this is not, I think, the intention of Mitchell's treatment of the issue. But what is clear is that if the Cosmological Argument (or rather the theistic solution of the cosmological problem) is to do anything at all, there must be signs of divine Creativity in the natural order. One possibility of this is expressed in the Argument from Design; here we begin with Aquinas' version, in the Fifth Way.

This way is "taken from the governance of the world." We see that beings not endowed with knowledge act for an end, as is evidenced by their acting always or nearly always in the same way. Thus they achieve their end not fortuitously, but designedly. But they cannot do this of their own accord, since they lack knowledge. Where something not endowed with knowledge achieves an end, it must be because it is governed by a rational agent—as the arrow is directed by the archer. So some intelligent being exists by whom all natural things are directed to their end; "and this being we call God."

It might be useful to call this version of the Teleological Argument the "Argument from Order." It seems to be the orderliness of the natural world which points to its purposiveness and thus its being directed by a supreme intelligence. The main form of the argument discussed by David Hume in his famous *Dialogues on Natural Religion* compares the universe more explicitly with a machine, and so its origin must surely lie in the mind of a Designer. This can be called "The Argument from Apparent Design" (see J. J. C. Smart's "The Existence of God" in *New Essays in Philosophical Theology* [6]). Another famous version of the argument is to be found in William Paley's *Natural Theology* [7] and other writings. Paley is here more concerned with particular examples of apparent design, such as the construction of the human eye, the way the teeth are providentially well-organised for mastication, and so on. We might call this aspect of the argument "The Argument from Instances of Apparent Design." This last form of the argument has lost much of its persuasiveness since the general acceptance of evolutionary theory, which gives an alternative naturalistic account of such instances, in terms of the survival of the fittest, etc.

There is also a pair of versions of the argument current in the Indian tradition, and criticised by Ramanuja penetratingly. (He anticipated many of Hume's arguments, and had others besides.) One version is rather similar to the Argument from Apparent Design, and tries to establish that the universe resembles an artifact. The other draws attention to the supposed resemblance of the universe to a living organism; but a living organism needs a soul. The soul of the cosmos directing it is God. A description of these important arguments and objections can be found in my *Doctrine and Argument in Indian Philosophy*. [8]

It must be noted that Aquinas' argument concludes with a single Governor of the world. This conclusion is only warranted by the premisses if the cosmos is considered as a single system of interlocking regularities. Otherwise, the regularity with which (say) the sun rises could at best be an argument for an intelligence governing the sun, and there is no need for this to be the same one that governs the moon. Thus orderliness is a property ascribed to the cosmos as a whole. Similarly the appeal in the Argument from Apparent Design to the likeness of the universe to a machine implies that we treat the cosmos as a single entity.

But this makes it look as though the Argument is not a scientific one, for science is to do with the connection of features internal to the cosmos, not with the explanation of the cosmos as a whole. However, the Argument from Apparent Design does operate "internally" to the cosmos in the following respect: it compares the whole of the cosmos to an item discoverable within it—the whole cosmos to a machine. But what are the grounds for thinking that the cosmos is really like a machine? What is a machine anyway?

A machine might be characterised as having three properties. First, it is artificial: it's made by human beings. Second, it has a relatively complex set of interlocking and moving parts. For this reason, we do not call a hoe a machine. Third, it is designed to do a job, like canning peas (or to do lots of jobs, if it is highly versatile; like some computers, which can be programmed to play chess, compose routine music, do the factory accounts, and solve problems in trigonometry). Its function is extrinsic to itself. For this reason, we do not call a mobile a machine.

How far are the three properties of a piece? Given a complex machine, can one infer its function or functions? Can one infer its being artificial? On the latter score, I think it reasonable to hold that one can infer that a given object is artificial from its appearance; but the inference is based on previous experience of what kinds of things human beings make. For example, if I come across something in the shape of a jellyfish on the seashore, but find that it is made of plastic, I can infer that this is a human creation. In making things, human beings characteristically reshape the materials that are found in nature. In short, by the very characteristic *difference* of the materials from natural materials I can infer that something is an artifact. It then is somewhat paradoxical to hold that the natural order resembles a machine. So if there is to be a case for the Argument from Apparent Design, the inference does not depend on reflection about the materials used. It must be the complexity of interlocking and moving parts that counts. Perhaps they are organised in such a way as to suggest a function which the whole has. (Or functions; the universe could be a versatile machine.)

How does one determine the function of a machine from inspecting it? Suppose I come across a mechanical reaper for the first time. I note that it has wheels, so it looks as if it is meant to move. I find out which direction by seeing that it has got arrangements for being hitched on to something else, it having no motive power of its own. There is also a fair amount of iron-work attached to it which doesn't help it to move, and even impedes its possible progress. From this I infer that the reaper is not in fact a carriage—the movement is subservient to a further end: it is not itself the main function. I note that the iron-work contains blades that cut. Obviously, they cannot cut anything very thick or hard. The width of the machine suggests that whatever is cut occurs densely, and over a fairly big area (otherwise why move?). I am already getting close to the idea that the machine is for cutting planted areas. If I then infer it is a reaper, it is because I have experience of phenomena such as wheat fields.

Part of the inference depends on seeing what bits of a machine subserve other bits; and part on previous experience of the way the world is, externally to the machine itself. It is hard to see how this latter aspect of such inferences could be used to diagnose the function or functions of the cosmos seen as a whole. The best, then, that one could do in contemplating the cosmos as possibly machinelike is to note first the complexity of its interlocking parts; and second the way in which some look as if they subserve others (as the wheels subserved the cutting in the reaper).

Let us grant that the universe can be seen as a complex, orderly, interlocking, moving whole. Does this enable us to say that it is really like a machine (and therefore presumably has a Designer)? But inspection of an organism also reveals that it is a complex, orderly, etc., thing. Is it not just as plausible to compare the cosmos to a fruitfly or a vegetable (the latter is Hume's example) as to a machine? Yet we do not think that a fruitfly has an intelligent Designer (unless we already believe in God); we do not need to think of a universe that is like a fruitfly as having been constructed by an intelligent agent. If the cosmos is like a machine, then since we know that a machine is an artifact it is plausible to think of the cosmos as a sort of artifact; but if it is like a fruitfly we have no reason in experience for thinking that it has been built by a Designer, for we have no ground to think that fruitflies are artifacts.

Further, even if the cosmos were an artifact, there is no reason to think there is a single Creator. The *Queen Mary*, for instance, splendid in its day as a well-integrated machine for transporting folk across the Atlantic and entertaining them on the way, had several thousand people involved in designing and building it. In human experience, indeed, the more complex an artifact is the more likely it has more than one builder.

So far, the Argument from Apparent Design does not look very convincing. In any event, the appearances of design are sufficiently vague and open to different subjective interpretations for us to liken the matter of seeing such design to discriminating animal and other shapes in the clouds. It is hard to see from the set-up of the cosmos a determinate function or set of functions that it might have as a huge machine.

We turn therefore to thinking of the problem posed by the Argument from Order. Does the existence of order itself somehow imply that the cosmos is an artifact? Why should it not be orderly? And for that matter, ought we not also to look at the signs of *disorder* in the cosmos? Not all events are regular: randomness, for instance, plays an important role in sub-atomic physics. Human behavior is not altogether regular and stereotyped. There are ways in which our environment seems messy. There are earthquakes; and what great regularity is there in meteorological phenomena? The world seems to be a mixture of recurrent themes and particularities; it is a mixture of the orderly and the accidental.

Why should the cosmos not be as orderly as it is? This question has a certain resemblance to another limiting question which we have encountered—as to why the cosmos exists at all. It is hardly likely (to say the least) that science can do more than point to some brute principles which account for the particular regularities which exist in the cosmos. We ever try to dig deeper below the surface of the given in experience, hoping to find fundamental principles which will serve to explain what at first sight seems inchoate and disorderly. For instance, meteorology is an attempt to deal with an unpromising set of observations, the capricious onsets of wet weather, the sudden storms, the overlong hot periods—the whole gamut of weather as we know it. It tries to show how even all this can be explained by reference to fundamental laws, together with the existing peculiarities of the earth, its surface, its atmosphere and so on. Still, it is not possible to deduce everything from what is self-evident. There must remain a contingency about the actual order in the world, however far we may advance in reducing it to a more comprehensible order.

We know that the world has a fair degree of orderliness; we think too that this will never be entirely explicable. For however far we reduce this orderliness to a more fundamental form, we can well conceive that the world might have been more disorderly than it is. It is possible to suppose that there was nothing solid in the cosmos, or rather in another possible cosmos. Randomness could play a strong part in macroscopic events as well as in sub-atomic ones. Things could have been altogether more chaotic than they are in fact. No doubt any cosmos would have to contain some laws, some inner regularities. But it need not be as orderly as our cosmos.

Why then should it be so? Do we here have a clue to the reason why Aquinas should have thought of orderliness as a sign of design? Well, only in so far as a certain degree of orderliness can be counted as such. As we have hinted, any cosmos would have some measure of order. And in any event, it scarcely looks as if regularity by itself shows that natural events are governed by a supreme intelligence. The question of why events should be regular (a limiting question) can as reasonably be countered by the limiting question in reverse: Why should they not be? If there is to be some kind of answer to the problem of why the cosmos is as orderly as it is (and this is only vaguely stated, for there are no precise measurements of orderliness), compared with other possibilities that we can envisage, it must be one which picks out some significant feature of the cosmos as exhibiting some function or purpose which such orderliness makes possible (and so subserves, like the wheels on the reaping machine).

It looks as if there could be no rational, conscious life unless there were a fair degree of regularity in our environment. Rationality requires some amount of reliance on the way the future is going to go. Life itself requires a fair degree of stability in natural laws and in the milieu in which it has to exist. So it could be argued that without the present amount of orderliness there could be no conscious life. Does this supply the beginnings of an answer to the question of why the cosmos is as orderly as it is? Only if one shifts conscious life into the center of the picture that attempts to discriminate the pattern of things. Treating it as the clue to the orderliness of the cosmos is analogous to treating religion as the central aspect of experience which thus is used to interpret the rest. But once again we are met with an ambiguous situation.

On the one hand there seems an attraction in treating conscious life as an important clue: it looks as if the evolutionary process reaches some kind of "higher flowering" in the emergence of man, and may still go higher. Such sentiments are expressed in the writings of Teilhard de Chardin, e.g., in *The Phenomenon of Man.*[9] There is much confusion in these writings, but they latch on to the feeling that somehow one can understand better evolution by seeing how it is likely to end up (just as one seems to understand better what an acorn is by seeing the oak that springs forth from it). After all, even from a philosophically materialist point of view, it could be argued that organisms and humans display new properties of matter that are not included within the purview of physics. It is as important to consider matter under its living, and even its rational, aspect, as it is to consider it under its "physical" aspect. So to understand matter one must see how it ends up on the evolutionary tree. These are interesting considerations, but surely they bear more on the way we should conceive the advance of the physical and biological science than on the religious significance (if any) of the emergence of man.

Moreover, though it is possible to see in that emergence (and also, doubtless in the emergence of rational creatures of other kinds elsewhere in the cosmos) some special significance, it also has to be noted that the cosmos is of immense scale—most of it being unpopulated by life. It looks simultaneously hospitable to living forms and unhospitable. Why pick on its hospitability as so significant? Why not equally draw attention to the ways in which the cosmos frustrates the emergence of life, and is, so to say, cruel to it once it does emerge here and there?

In sum, it is not easy to fix on any version of the Teleological Argument which is persuasive. The best that it can do is to draw attention to the relative orderliness of the cosmos, and thereby its relative hospitability to life. It is two-faced, from the point of view of limiting questions. On the one hand, it shows itself as yielding life, and consciousness, and with all that the colors and shapes that would never be apparent to blind atoms. On the other hand, it shows itself as prodigal and reckless of the little life that exists in its vast reaches.

It is not quite absurd to answer the limiting question about the orderliness of the cosmos in terms of the significance of the living manifestations of matter which that orderliness makes possible. But it is only one picture of the world. Therefore, we can simultaneously explain the grip which the Teleological Argument can retain even on those (such as Immanuel Kant) who have rejected its logic and the defects which it has as an argument. The grip has to do with the way in which the cosmos can be pictured as "friendly" to consciousness; the weakness can be explained by the possibility of alternative pictures of the world arising from the contemplation of the orderliness of it, in relation to the emergence of life.

The grip it has is reinforced by aesthetic considerations. Kant referred to the starry skies above and the moral law within as inducing religious feelings. It is not, though, only the starry skies that bring a sense of awe and beauty. The world is indeed beautiful (though ugly too), and in the deepest moments of contemplation induces a sense of giddiness at its wonders. Yet we reflect easily enough that beauty and wonder mean nothing without those to contemplate it. The austerity of Gauguin in painting for the sake of painting, but not at all of showing, is almost unintelligible. "Almost"—for after all there was Gauguin painting. But suppose we built a Gauguin machine that could turn out as good paintings, and we set it in a hut in the South Pacific, churning out masterpieces that no-one, not even the machine itself, could ever see?

The aesthetic sense of the wonder and beauty of the world itself can generate another version of the Teleological Argument, where the cosmos is not compared to a machine, but to a work of art. Behind it perhaps there is the great Artist. It is hard, though, to know what criteria should be employed here; for we are in enough difficulty about mundane works of art, especially in these latter, zanier days. And what if the world should be judged a poor work of art?

For the world to be analogous to revelation or what is given in religion, it would neither have to be purely machine-like nor purely painting-like. It would have to display signs of mystery, of holiness.

This is perhaps why the starry skies above could thus impress Kant—they induce more than a sense of beauty; but also a sense of awe and reverence (as did the moral law within, with its capacity to override our wishes and bring about a sense of humility).

So, if we are diagnosing the grip that the Teleological Argument can have, despite its defects as classically presented, we could explain it as follows. The question of the orderliness of the cosmos is a limiting question that goes beyond the possibilities of a properly scientific answer; but it invites us to ask why the cosmos is as orderly as it is. One possible answer is that thereby it allows conscious life. In this we may see the "point" of the whole, the most significant flowering of the mutifarious forms of matter. But at the same time, the cosmos displays itself to us as beautiful, awe-inspiring, and mysterious. (It also displays itself to us under the aspect of colors and shapes and smells, etc.: an aspect that could not be but for us and like beings—is the table brown in itself?) Its strangeness and beauty could not manifest itself if there were no living matter. So the Teleological Argument, by a devious route, arouses in us the sense that the "meaning" (the living meaning) of the cosmos is found in the way its orderliness makes possible conscious life and the reflection therein of its beauties and mysteries.

This cannot pretend to be in one sense a rational, persuasive argument. It is just the presentation of a possible picture of life, which may be reinforced from other directions (for instance, the sense of providence in the joys and sufferings of individual existence). The picture helps to answer another limiting question. It "makes sense" of the problems posed jointly by the Cosmological and Teleological Arguments. But it only does so if there is something to connect up the possible picture with actuality. That cannot be supplied by natural theology alone. Taken in conjunction with the "given," the picture presented as one solution to the problems posed makes some sense. Taken in isolation, it is a merely speculative and thin account of how the world might be. By still another route we arrive at the conclusion that natural theology may provide reasons for seeing the cosmos in the light of more particular manifestations of the religious ultimate; but it cannot stand on its own feet. It allows too many loopholes.

It allows the loophole of agnosticism about the answers to the

limiting questions. It even allows a loophole in experience. The
world does not always seem mysterious and beautiful. Its contingency does not only arouse the feeling of awe. There is also the
possibility of nausea, well described by Jean-Paul Sartre (I quote
from Mary Warnock's translation of *La Nausée* in her *The Philosophy of Sartre*):

> The Nausea hasn't left me and I think it will be some time be-
> fore it does; but I don't suffer from it any more, it is no longer an
> illness or a passing fit: it is I.
> For instance, I was in the public park just now. The horse-
> chestnut root went down into the ground just under my bench. I
> could no longer remember that it was a root. The words had van-
> ished and with them the meaning of things, their uses, the signifi-
> cant points of reference that men have traced on their surfaces. I
> was sitting alone, stooping a little, with my head bowed, alone in
> the face of this black, knotted, crude mass which frightened me.
> And then I had a sudden illumination.
> It took my breath away. I had never, until these last few days,
> suspected what "to exist" meant . . . And without formulating
> anything clearly I realised that I had discovered the key to Exist-
> ence, the key to my fits of Nausea and the key to my own life.
> Indeed, anything that I have managed to apprehend since leads
> back to the same basic absurdity. "Absurdity": another word: I
> fight against words: down there in the park I touched the
> thing . . .
>
>   .   .   .
>
> To exist is simply *to be there*: existing things appear, let them-
> selves be encountered, but one can never *deduce* them. I think
> there are people who have understood this. Only they tried to
> overcome contingency by inventing a necessary being, a self-caused
> cause. Now no necessary being can explain existence: contingency
> isn't an illusion or a mere appearance that can be dissipated; it is
> the absolute, and thus the perfect inconsequent: everything is
> inconsequential, the park, the town and myself . . .[10]

There is in Sartre's experience here described a combination of a
powerful, almost mystical sense of the sheer bruteness of existence
and a strong intimation that the human way of looking at the world
is a kind of anthropomorphism. The world is alien to human values;

and it is projection and a deceit to think otherwise. This is the main, and in a way more heroic, alternative way of picturing the world. Perhaps that is why we tend to respect more representations of the Creator which are not comforting to human egoism, and also bring out something of the absurdity of his predicament—representations which portray God as challenging human values, as with the God of the Old Testament, or as being "beyond" them, as with the multiple representations of Shiva, both Creator and Destroyer, both merciful and fierce. This is perhaps why also the nausea of Sartre and the numinous experience are like two sides of the same coin. There is a kind of brutish mystery in the encounter with the Holy, which cannot be explained away—a reason why Otto used the term "non-rational" to describe this category of experience.

In brief, then, it does not seem that the Cosmological and Teleological Arguments can be counted as proofs of God's existence. The best they can do is present limiting questions about the existence and orderliness of the cosmos as a whole. These questions express problems about the world, which can find one kind of solution in religious belief. But there remains a loophole of agnosticism and even of positive "nausea" with the absurdity of existence. Yet the so-called proofs at least lead us to a way in which the world can not irrationally be seen as created and providentially ordered, given that we begin at one side from what is given in religion.

But this implies, to repeat a point insisted on earlier, that the so-called proofs are only of relevance in theistic faiths and their analogues. It is unlikely, to say the least, that they could have any power for, say, the Buddhist, who does not begin with a picture of the manifestation of the religious ultimate which could be extended in *this* way to the world of nature. His mode of understanding the latter is rather different, though also analogous. Thus the sense of impermanence of ordinary existence accruing upon the encounter with the Permanent (nirvana) is extended to the ordinary world through arguments, not to establish the existence of God, etc., but to show that things are in fact made up of short-lived events, etc. His "natural theology" is more in the form of a "natural metaphysics." This is not to say that because the presupposed starting points in the given differ and so the arguments, the latter are without force. They do have some force; but they can only gain a clinching position when they start from a religious base. Otherwise they become both weak and irrelevant. Let us illustrate with a rather faint parallel.

I suspect that a solicitor friend of mine is embezzling money. I think I have evidence because he has just bought a Rolls-Royce, which typically he would not be able to afford. By itself, though, this fact amounts to nothing much. If I start from something firmer —some suspicious remarks, some guilty looks, some knowledge of his opportunities, some curious transactions at the bank: then the Rolls-Royce can be used as an argument, but otherwise it is of little importance. So, it can be thought, the problems posed by natural theology and natural metaphysics do not point very clearly to any particular solutions of them.

One other main feature of the arguments is worth noting. It was pointed out that if they were to work at all they would have to be about the cosmos considered as a whole: they have to begin by taking the form of limiting questions in relation to science. They are in this sense extra-scientific problems that they pose. This is important for two reasons.

The first is that it is commonly thought that there is some kind of conflict between religion and science. This is both true and false. There can be competition only if they both play in the same league. In so far, however, as religious beliefs present solutions to limiting questions, they do not play in the same league. Further, such categories as that of the Holy do not belong to scientific discourse; and the whole characterisation of the manifestations of the religious ultimate given in previous Chapters should surely make it extraordinary to suppose that *these* were intended as contributions to scientific investigation. Thus in general religion and science do not play in the same league. Hence the "extra-scientific" character of the solutions to the questions posed by the arguments should not disturb us—indeed it is encouraging that it is so, for it shows that those who have debated these arguments, for and against, have (if often, it is true) confusedly, debated them in the right spirit.

It is still true that in actuality there has been conflict between some scientists and some religious apologists. Such conflict was notable in the last Century, when the theory of evolution was sometimes taken to be a challenge to the truth of *Genesis* (not that the latter looks much like a textbook in biology). This clash was partly the consequence of a literalist, deductivist interpretation of the scriptures. This itself had some more ancient roots, for the scriptures were written in a prescientific age, and so take no account of how they are to be interpreted or reinterpreted with advances in human knowledge. It is certainly therefore possible for religion to commit itself to positions in which it *does* play in the same league as science (and typically is heavily defeated: is there a converse to this?). One of the tasks of philosophy, and the philosophy of religion in particular, is to give a characterisation of religion in its relation to science which will clarify the essential nature of religious concepts. It thus may help to dispel a kind of literalism which confuses categories, in effect. (On the other hand, it remains a question as to how much substance religious belief has drawn in the past from pseudo-science and pseudo-history—some people believe that if you take away all the literal claims of this kind, say about the miraculous crossing of the Red Sea or the temptation of the first man in the Garden of Eden, religious utterances will be left devoid of substance. However, I think the characterisation we have given in the first few Chapters may dispel this illusion. This is not to say, to repeat, that some religion or other must be true; all faiths may rest on illusion; but one must at least see what they are, how their concepts work.)

So far, then, there is no necessary clash between science and religion. If one is to look at the developments of the last hundred years or so of the increased scepticism in certain Western countries of the influence of religion, it has less to do with the supposed "unscientific" character of religious belief than with moral and social criticisms of religion. Moreover, the application of historical criticism to the scriptures has played a part in scepticism and doubt. These are, of course, historical comments on the way things have gone; though they also point to the complexity not only of religious beliefs themselves, but of the response to them in a crucial period of Western history.

I mention "Western" history here because it is a fallacy to suppose that intellectual and practical problems challenge religions in the same way. The impact of evolutionary theory on Hinduism and Buddhism, for example, has been much less than on Christianity and

Judaism. It was always part of the world-picture of Indian religions that the cosmos was vast, indeed infinite: there was no problem about scholars tracing its origin to such a laughably small figure as 4004 B.C. There was no essential split in thinking between the world of man and the world of the animals. It was no insult for men to be descended from monkeys. The doctrine of rebirth made nonsense of the psychological trauma caused by Darwin. I mention the psychological trauma, because it is always worth asking the question of why a particular doctrine or theory should be resisted so fiercely: it often turns out that the motives do not so much have to do with arguments as with deep-seated feelings. The reaction of many people in the Victorian middle class to the idea that men might be descended from animals is therefore psychologically and even sociologically interesting. People in the West had been brought up on a long tradition (not, as it happens, totally scriptural) of the great divide between men and animals. The language of most people had built into it a suggestion that various wicked activities, including sexual activities (which are not in themselves, from most religious points of view, wicked), are bestial, animal, beastly (note how the vocabulary of abuse draws on the animal kingdom). It was thus a great psychological shock that there should be scientific evidence of human descent from the animals. This can account for some of the ferocity of reaction. This, coupled with scriptural literalism, is sufficient to explain the nineteenth-century conflict over evolution, between churchmen (or rather only some churchmen: many supported Darwin) and scientists (or rather some scientists: many were conservative enough to be sceptical of Darwin—and rightly in a way, though on occasion for the wrong reasons, for science flourishes on criticism, even conservative criticism).

In fact, the possibilities of conflict between science and religion depend on two things. One is the literalism of a faith; the other is its shape. It is a fallacy to think that there is a single problem of the relation between science and religion. Thus, Christianity has traditionally put much more emphasis than, say, Judaism, on the Fall: the Fall seems to imply a first (representative) man. No such can be confidently discovered by biological and paleontological research. Well, that is a problem for those who take *Genesis* in a rather literal way. But the same problem does not afflict Buddhism. Other problems of the relation between science and religion arise. In short, the problems depend on the several shapes of belief. For example, Buddhism as traditionally presented involves belief in rebirth. This means that when I die (and I consist in a series of mental and physical states), the series constituting myself will give rise to a further series. Now at first sight this presents a scientific, not just a religious or spiritual, problem. For if somehow at my death the present (Smart) series gives rise to another, there must be a causal connection between the two. This indeed is part of the Buddhist thesis. But then how do we account for the situation created by modern genetics? Suppose I am reborn as a girl in Madagascar. She has parents. According to modern genetics, her character and appearance, etc., derive from the genes of the parents. How then can her career be somehow determined by the fact that I am her predecessor in the chain of existence? The ancient doctrine of rebirth (reincarnation, metempsychosis, transmigration—different terms have been used for it, à propos of a very widespread and differently expressed belief among people of different cultures, ranging from ancient Greece to India) appears to conflict with modern science. Yet it was not produced in the context of modern science. It has the ambiguity of mythic thinking: what is one to say about it when differentiations are made which do not occur in the cultures producing it? Yet what can be done for God can be done for rebirth. In regard to the Creation a distinction is made between scientific questions about the cosmos and metaphysical ones. So likewise it can be argued, as it has been by some, such as the philosopher John M. E. McTaggart in *Some Dogmas of Religion*,[11] that when A dies, his soul (or karma, it matters not how we describe the trend towards rebirth) "homes" on suitable parents. This account evades the genetic objection, by making the doctrine of rebirth metaphysical.

It is hard to see how such considerations have much relevance to the Christian faith. But they have relevance to Buddhism, etc. We note that somewhat similar methods of argument are used: the essence of the belief, whether Christian or Buddhist for example, is not intended as scientific or as open to scientific falsification. Yet despite the similarity of form in reply, the content of the discussion clearly owes very much to the content of the religion in question (also to the branch of science in question). For this reason, it is absurd to speak of *the* problem of the relation between religion and science. There are many. There are some tenets of religion which are liable to swift scientific refutation. There are others which seem to preserve more deeply the inner meaning of faith.

One other point about the relation between religion and science needs to be made. So far we have looked at what might be called "substantive scientism"—i.e., there are particular reasons why it is best to look for scientific answers to all questions of fact. From this point of view, religion is false in that it makes particular claims which can perhaps be shown on scientific grounds to be false. But there is a deeper form of scientism, which can be called "philosophical scientism," namely the view that all questions of fact can in principle be resolved scientifically: there is therefore no question of some kind of transcendental truth which lies beyond the scope of scientific enquiry.

Such a scientism is quite an important aspect of contemporary folklore. It found sophisticated expression in A. J. Ayer's *Language, Truth, and Logic* [12] and in the movement known in general as Logical Positivism (of which Ayer's book was essentially a part). But this sort of scientism is in one way not at all scientific. It is about the scope of science, not about anything within science. It describes its boundaries (as coterminous with the boundaries of what can properly be called facts). It is thus a philosophical doctrine. It may be right. But it should not be given the accolade of being dubbed "scientific" because it is about science—any more than the philosophy of religion should be called religious. Questions about the possible range of facts (alternatively, about the possible varieties of language which can enshrine truths, etc.) are essentially philosophical questions. They are also in a way boundary questions: for how could any scientific experiment, observation, or theory determine whether there is in principle something which lies beyond the bounds of experiment, observation, and scientific theory?

In brief, philosophical scientism really is philosophical. The issue is not an issue in science. If it is said that there is conflict between religion and science because science is the final arbiter of fact, then this is no longer an issue between religion and science as such. It is an issue between religion and philosophical scientism. It becomes therefore a philosophical dispute. I do not here propose to say any more about it than this: if religion is at all persuasive (and it may not be) philosophical scientism is false. We have sufficiently discussed the other issues about religious truth and falsity. And yet, it will be replied, more should be said about the human sciences. Scientism is so commonly stated in physicists' terms. But does not the growth of psychology (for example), suggest that there can be a natural explanation of religious experience? If so, there is a major manifestation of the religious ultimate which seemingly can be "explained away."

Though philosophical scientism in its general form is a dubitable doctrine, there surely is force in the thought that increasingly scientific methods are tending to explain various kinds of phenomena, including human ones. If that is so, there seems a diminishing role for appeal to special and even miraculous accounts of divine "intervention" in human experience. It is not so much that people have a preconceived philosophy. Is it not rather that they are tending to replace older religious explanations with more up-to-date scientific ones? And these, of course, include psychological ones.

To a discussion of these issues I now turn. No-one can deny the immense impact which modern psychology has made on the current thinking of our times.

But first, to sum up briefly on the preceding discussion: the so-called "proofs" of God's existence look more like modes of raising problems about the cosmos as a whole. One sort of solution is given by religion, but it is not mandatory. The questions are limiting ones, so the answers are extra-scientific. Religion and science should not, it seems, play in the same league; though they have sometimes done so. The next Chapter will reveal whether after all they do need to play in the same league. If so, the answer, truth-wise, can probably be predicted. But if not . . .

Notes

1. Ninian Smart, *Doctrine and Argument in Indian Philosophy* (New York: Humanities, 1964), Chap. 9.
2. Bishop Butler, *Analogy of Religion*. Extracts from Bishop But-

ler's book are reproduced in Ninian Smart, *Historical Selections in the Philosophy of Religion* (New York: Harper & Row, 1962).

3. Frederick R. Tennant, *Philosophical Theology* (Cambridge: Cambridge University Press), Vol. II, Chap. 7. This chapter is reprinted in Smart, *Historical Selections . . .* , *op. cit.*, pp. 465 ff.

4. Basil Mitchell, in Antony Flew and Alasdair MacIntyre, *New Essays in Philosophical Theology* (New York: Macmillan).

5. *Ibid.*, p. 105.

6. See J. J. C. Smart, "The Existence of God," in Flew and MacIntyre, *op. cit.*, p. 42.

7. William Paley, *Natural Theology* (Indianapolis: Bobbs-Merrill).

8. Smart, *Doctrine and Argument . . .* , *op. cit.*

9. See, for example, Teilhard de Chardin, *The Phenomenon of Man* (New York: Harper & Row).

10. This passage is quoted from Mary Warnock's translation of *La Nausée* in *The Philosophy of Sartre* (New York: Hillary), pp. 90 ff.

11. John M. E. McTaggart, *Some Dogmas of Religion* (New York: Kraus Reprint Corp.).

12. A. J. Ayer, *Language, Truth, and Logic* (New York: Dover).

Chapter Six ✺

✺ ✺ ✺ On Some Theories of Religion

It has been argued that religious systems very much start from the given, and in so far as they have something to say about the natural world, this is in the shape of solutions to limiting questions. Consequently, there is reason to think that religion and science involve distinct criteria and forms of expression, and so do not need to be in conflict. But it is not hard to see that a series of question-marks may hang over the "given." What use is it to dwell on Paul's conversion as a ground for faith in Christ's resurrection and capacity to redeem if that conversion can be given a straightforward psychological explanation? How can one contentedly begin from a tradition that depicts God as a Father when there is the uneasy feeling that this imagery has its roots in childhood experience and conflicts? May it not be the case that the whole of what I have called the "given" in religion is explicable in terms of psychological projections upon the hard, real world?

Still, what if it is? A moving experience would still remain a moving experience; a conversion would still remain a conversion; the peace of God would still be peace. Yes, but would it be *of God?* The thought lying behind the above unease is not that somehow religion as a phenomenon would be conjured away: how could it be? It exists. It is rather that what are taken as manifestations of the religious ultimate are not really that at all, but simply the consequences of certain preceding natural states. What is being called in question is not the existence of religious experiences and mythic forms of expression, but the validity of these.

By "validity" presumably something like this is meant: if a person has an experience interpreted by him as being an experience of God (nirvana, etc.), it is valid if and only if it really is an experience of God (etc.). Stated in this way, the problem becomes a highly complex one. For what is meant by *God*, for instance? If we take it in its rich form as presented in a whole religious scheme, one would have to show the truth of the whole scheme before an experience would have a chance of being valid. We might then settle for something a bit looser: an experience of X is valid if and only if it really is an experience of X or at least something like X. This would allow the Christian, say, to admit the validity of some Hindu experiences of God without being committed to the acceptance of the whole of the Hindu theology believed by the person having the experience.

But what is the ground for thinking that some psychological explanation of such an experience would affect its validity? As we shall see, this matter too is a more difficult one than appears at first sight. But the feeling behind this thought of a threat to religion from psychology is doubtless this—that a valid experience of X must somehow proceed from X. Consider the following example.

I am looking at a fig tree. Suppose a clever physiologist explains to me the whole process whereby I have sensations of green, etc., this does not shake my faith that I really am looking at a fig tree. Do I not reckon that light is bouncing off the tree and impinging on my retina? Is it not the case that there is a causal transaction between the fig tree and me? On the other hand, if I seem to be looking at some pink rats, I might feel unease. Could it not be that there is no particular group of things out there producing effects in my eyes and brain, but rather that the whisky bottle is the cause of my sensations? So it looks as though a valid perception is one where the X I perceive has special causal effects on me. This at least seems to be a *necessary* condition of validity of perception.

We now see why a psychological account of religious experience is disturbing. For it seems to offer an account of an experience of X which renders superfluous any account in terms of the causal effects of X on the person having the experience. If the experience can perfectly well be explained without having recourse to a causal relation between X and the experience of X, there is no ground for thinking the experience to be valid.

Once this model has taken a grip, there seems no way of stopping it from complete domination of the discussion. For even if it were shown that particular attempts (e.g., Freudian ones) to explain religious experience were inadequate, it still remains possible to say: But one day we'll come up with a good explanation. However many particular psychological theories were knocked down, there would always be some more waiting for discovery. The thesis that no religious experience is valid because in principle explainable psychologically would thus be unfalsifiable (a sad state of affairs, if we take modern empiricism seriously, and the falsifiability criterion of scientific hypotheses). The situation becomes like that in relation to the free-will controversy. The view that all human acts are in principle explicable in terms of prior causes (determinism) becomes irrefutable. For if I come up with an act which cannot, as a matter of fact be so explained satisfactorily, the reply is, but one day perhaps we will be able to do this.

But would not the defender of free will be in equal trouble if he claimed that there will always be some acts which are not in principle explicable? Even if some of the candidates he puts forward turn out to be rather useless, and indeed explainable quite satisfactorily, he can always hope to produce some better ones. But this way of going about it betrays the weakness of his position. For his claim to have any substance he must be able to say very roughly at least what kind of acts are inexplicable, and if some falling under this category turn out to be determined, there is some presumption that other future candidates will prove equally ineffective. Putting the matter another way: though determinism taken in the way indicated above is unfalsifiable, it has grounds in its favor, because of the increasing success of scientific psychology and physiology in tracing the causes of human actions. If, then, the proponent of free-will is to be successful, he must produce some well-backed theoretical reasons why certain sorts of actions could not be totally explained causally. (This would be like the way it can be shown on theoretical grounds that certain observations, e.g., simultaneous knowledge of the position and velocity of an electron, are impossible, and not because of a technical inadequacy in the measuring instruments, etc.)   Attempts at such philosophical and theoretical accounts of the impossibility of establishing causal determinism have been made, e.g., by R. S. Peters in his *The Concept of Motivation,* and by myself in *Philosophers and Religious Truth*.[1]   Whether these are successful is another matter.

Transferring this discussion now to the psychology of religious experience, the claim to plausibility of what we may call "Religious Naturalism," i.e., the thesis that religious experience can be explained psychologically, would rest on the degree to which psychology shows signs of being successful in such explanations.   As we shall see, not much has yet been done, though there are one or two suggestive diagnoses, amid a lot of often speculative and odd interpretations of religion.   But even though the psychology of religion may not have met with too much genuine success to date, it can still be argued that these are early days, and there are at least some signs of the fruitfulness of the attempt at naturalistic psychological explanations.

However, we need to look critically at the assumption that such explanations do in fact impugn the validity of the experiences, in the way suggested earlier.   Here we meet a host of complications, and it is best to begin with one which is relevant to the case of theism. Suppose it can be shown that a religious experience of mine can be traced back to some childhood events, together with precipitating factors in my present life.   Let us call these causes the NF ("natural factors").   Does the fact that my experience is caused by NF militate against the claim that it was caused by God?   Is not God, as continuous creator and sustainer of the world not the cause of the NF themselves?   So the assumption that a naturalistic explanation conflicts with a divine one is unwarranted.

It looks as if there was a secret thesis underlying the assumption, namely that all manifestations of the religious ultimate must be supernatural and miraculous in character—irruptions, as it were, into the ordinary fabric of events.   To show then that there is a natural explanation is *ipso facto* to show that there is no irruption, and hence that there is no genuine manifestation of the religious ultimate.   It is not just that an experience has to be caused by God to be a valid one: it must be miraculously caused.

There is perhaps some warrant for this secret thesis.   After all, religions often treasure the miraculous and gape at what is thought to be supernatural. The "God of the gaps" keeps recurring—the one who is brought in to "explain" what has hitherto defeated scientific explanation. Nevertheless, the secret thesis requires scrutiny.

What would count as a miraculous irruption into the ordinary fabric of events? To be incompatible with a naturalistic explanation, a divine or supernatural one would at least not have to be natural! But what then counts as a naturalistic explanation? There is perhaps here a confusion between two criteria which might be used. One is an ontological criterion; the other a methodological one.

Ontologically, it is tempting to make a distinction between two orders of events, etc., natural and supernatural ones. The latter are somehow directly connected with a "higher" order of existence, lying "beyond" the natural world. This distinction is tempting, in view of much of religious language, which seems to split reality in this way. In earlier Chapters moreover we were at great pains to investigate the idea of the transcendent religious ultimate lying beyond its manifestations in the world.

Methodologically, one can use "naturalistic explanation" not to mean some explanation which refers to natural events, etc., but rather an explanation framed in accordance with scientific method. But this by itself, surely does not pick out any particular ontological realm. The world is the way it is, and may contain all sorts of facets. It is not as if the way I go about investigating it determines what it is like. Let us use an analogy.

Suppose I teach a small boy how to use a telescope. He learns a new way of observing things. But the method he uses does not determine the kinds of things he sees; they may be green or yellow, cows or candlesticks, stars or fleas. It does not pick out a special realm of objects, not picked out by sight itself. The new method of seeing does not by itself determine what kind of things are seen. There is no reason thus to think that the application of the scientific method by itself somehow delineates a special range of objects, namely natural ones.

The feeling that it does arises from two roots. One is that the most powerful and seminal branch of science, physics, was commonly regarded as the investigation of *nature*—indeed the phrase "natural philosophy" is still used in some ancient universities as a title for physics. And the concept of nature involved some kind of contrast with man. "Nature" meant man's environment, and more particularly the non-artificial natural environment. We still talk thus, in speaking of the beauties of nature (usually thought of as the immediate mundane environment of man, rather than the cosmos). It was some time before the biological sciences, including the investigation of man himself, came to be assimilated to the natural sciences. This rather special flavor to the term "nature" suggested there was a particular realm which science investigates. One still finds this dualism in some modern existentialist thinking: the sphere of science is the "objective" world; the sphere of existentialist psychology is the "subjective" (human) realm.

The other root of the feeling that there is a special realm of reality picked out by the scientific method is the reflection that perhaps the method itself is like a net of a certain mesh. It catches some of the fish, but not the smallest ones. So the application of science is important for understanding some aspects of the world, but there must be others which elude it. But it must be remembered that science is able to change: it may be, for instance, that behavioristic psychology only catches some of the psychological fish. But psychology is not tied down to behaviorism; it can employ scientific methods even though using introspective material, as reported from the conscious states lying behind behavior. Thus a lot of interesting research has been done in the last decade on dreams—correlating dreaming periods with minute twitching of the eyeballs, etc. Obviously, this involves more than the correlation of bits of behavior.

It is thus not at all necessary that the scope of scientific method and the "natural" world should coincide. It is best therefore to drop the term "naturalistic," in regard to psychological explanations of religious experience. If then it is *still* supposed that there is a conflict between such explanations and treating religious experiences as having a divine cause, it must be that the latter are thought of simply as inexplicable. But this is paradoxical, for is not assigning an experience to a divine cause giving some sort of explanation?

It is difficult, therefore, to give a coherent account of why in principle there is some conflict between the claim that a religious experience is valid and the claim that it can have a psychological explanation, at least in the context of theism. It happens that a certain difficulty arises in relation to one or two non-theistic systems. To this I shall come in a moment. Meanwhile, though, two points about explanations of religious experience need to be made.

First, as was mentioned earlier, some explanations can be "deflationary": it is not so much the fact that they are explanations which impugns the validity of the experience, but rather, the sort of explanations they are. If certain sorts of religion are, for instance, diagnosed as the result of failing to solve living problems, as infantile, as due to epilepsy or whatever, there is created a presumption that they are not as blessed as they claim.

Second, it looks a fair guess that if an experience can be explained it can in due course be manipulated: it would, to put the matter rather extremely, be possible to create visions of Krishna to order. But this suggests salvation by works than by the grace of God. It seems to run contrary to the emphasis in, for instance, Christian theism on the divine initiative. (Consider our earlier discussion of Barthian revelationism.) There has sometimes been a Protestant suspicion of contemplative mysticism, on the ground that it seems to be a method of achieving encounter with God, when there can be no such human method. However, the science fiction picture of a real possibility of manipulating the numinous does not seem altogether realistic. The guess is not as fair as it looks, for two reasons briefly. First, in religion as elsewhere in human culture there are many moments of creative originality. These cannot be produced by formula. Second, explanations would often have in a strong sense to be historical, i.e., concerned with the particular living circumstances of an individual's supposed encounter with God. By the same token the technology would have to be historical and individual in application. It would be like psycho-analysis, which has to adapt its methods to each patient. But then it should not surprise that there could be *this* sort of technology of encounter with God. Is this not the sort of thing spiritual directors attempt to do? It may only be that with increasing insight, such spiritual direction will become deeper and more effective.

The case of Buddhist nirvana appears different from the case of theism. For it was argued earlier that after all the theist could claim that his experience of God is (like everything else) caused by God. But in the Theravadin tradition there is no question of nirvana's

being an underlying something which might be said to be the cause
or ground of all events in the world. Does not then some explanation of the "seeing" of nirvana in terms of preceding natural factors
compete with the explanation that it is an experience due to nirvana
itself? (The matter is hard to state properly, since nirvana is not a
thing but a permanent, transcendent state.) Let us oversimplify the
problem by thinking of certain facets of a Buddhist saint's behavior
—his serenity, non-attachment, etc.—as being themselves caused by
the nirvana-experience. This is an oversimplification because they
are part of what constitutes the state of having attained nirvana;
because the model suggested is mechanistic (The validity of the idea
of causation needs examination in psychology and human behavior
—some rather more sophisticated, less mechanistic term may be
needed.); and for other reasons. But if we state the problem in these
terms, we might expect to discover the following conflict. While the
psychologist claims to explain the nirvana-experience by reference to
preceding NF, and so the serenity, etc., by reference to these same
NF, the Buddhist wishes to explain the serenity, etc., by reference to
the nirvana-experience, and so not solely by reference to the NF.

But why this last clause? What is the point at issue? Surely
neither party denies the occurrence of the nirvana-experience. The
obscurely felt divergence is that the Buddhist thinks of nirvana as, so
to say, really being there to be seen, and as being unconditioned,
uncaused (as the Buddha said). So the Buddhist sees the nirvana-
experience as a manifestation of a transcendent state, not just as the
product of the NF.

An analogy might be drawn from perception, again. If there is to
be an effective account of my present sensations, the state of my
environment has to be described. It is one of the reasons why I now
see something green that there is a fig-tree over there. Is it not then
that one of the reasons for the nirvana-experience is that there really
is a transcendent state to be perceived? But what are the criteria of
its reality? The issue is surely not settled by tracing out the NF
which give rise to the nirvana-experience. We might characterise the
divergence between the two accounts above as rather a difference
about how to describe reality. On the Buddhist description, reality
consists both of impermanent states, etc., and of a transcendent state;
on the other description, it consists solely of the former. We are

faced, it seems, with a situation like that pointed to by the garden parable.

But in discussing theistic experiences, we made mention of the criterion of whether an experience is caused by its object. Should this not be used here? Is not the test of whether the nirvana-experience is valid the possibility of isolating out nirvana as its cause? If the NF account for it, there seems to be a disproof of nirvana as cause.

But one must look more closely into what "account" means here. I think we would accept the following as an account in terms of NF disproving one sort of supernaturalistic explanation. Suppose I dream of an animal with a horse's head, a lion's body, a cow's tail, etc.; and suppose I am naïve enough to think that since I have never encountered such a beast, my dream must be a supernatural revelation—then an account which shows how elements of my experience have been put together in a disjointed way for intelligible reasons (e.g., the symbolic functions of the different animals in question) is a reasonable disproof of my naïve conclusion. Part of the question, then, about the nirvana-experience is whether it can be shown as deriving its components from previous elements of experience. Or is it rather like a piece of Mozart, containing something genuinely new in relation to the past of music? If there is something not thus reducible about the nirvana-experience, the explanation of its arising from NF does not show that there is no transcendent state of nirvana waiting (so to say) to be seen in the nirvana-experience. (Similar remarks apply to the experience of the Holy.) I do not myself believe that a reductionist account of the nirvana-experience can be given. But this is not a matter which can be determined *a priori*. Moreover, it should be noted that the *sui generis* character of nirvana would not establish the reality of transcendent nirvana, but belief in this would of course remain a live option.

Thus it is hard to see that the explicability of a religious experience by itself would affect its validity. Only when the explanation was either reductionist or deflationary would there be a ground for doubting validity (though not always, since on the theistic view, an experience reducible into prior components could still be sent to me providentially, God being the cause of everything). Thus if scepticism about religious claims occurs because of psychological, sociological and other theories of religion, it is because of their particular tendency to deflate or reduce. There is then no way of settling the issue save by looking at what theories have been offered. I want briefly to discuss three theories of religion, two drawn from psychology and one from sociology. This is of course a minute sample, though as it happens an influential one. I want to consider the theories of Freud, Jung, and Durkheim.

Freud's account of religion was partly historical—an attempt to diagnose the historical origins of religion in terms of psycho-analytic thinking—and partly psychological—to do with the way religion functions here and now. Unfortunately, his excursions into history in *Totem and Taboo* [2] and in *Moses and Monotheism* [3] are not altogether happy. In the former, he was too impressed by then current theories of totemism as being a key to the understanding of religion, and of the idea of the existence of a primal horde, so far without moral prohibitions, as being the first stage of prehistory. He linked these speculations to his own work on the Oedipus complex, and so reconstructed primeval events as follows. The father, the dominant male of the group, with the females in his power, excites the jealousy of the sons, who band together and kill him, and then eat his flesh (to partake thus of his power). In killing him, they are repeating in adulthood the jealousy of the father in the earliest stages of childhood. And they thereby create a sense of guilt. When later experience shows the chaos resulting from each brother's attempts to take over the father's place, a taboo on incest is created: a man must marry outside his clan or family group. The memory of the father (now seen to be the original founder of morality, for his actions corresponded to the taboo) is no longer conscious: it has been repressed because of the guilt associated with his killing. But it is maintained symbolically in the ritual eating of the totemic animal— an animal associated symbolically with the group and normally taboo, though to be killed and eaten on well-defined sacramental occasions. These are the distant origins, then, of morality, and explain the authority of the Father figure as demanding obedience to his laws. This authority and power rests on the guilt feelings arising from the Oedipus complex.

In *Moses and Monotheism*, Freud is perhaps even more speculative. He applies some of the foregoing ideas to the problem of the origins of Judaeo-Christian monotheism. Freud held that Moses was in fact killed by his followers during the Exodus, and that the monotheism he taught was given up for a time. The fact of his death was repressed, but eventually reemerged from the unconscious in the form of prophetic religion and a national neurosis, in which monotheism was reestablished. Hence the later force of Christianity: the death of Christ is an atonement for the death of the Father. The Eucharistic meal is also suggestive of the totemic ritual described in the previous book.

These very brief accounts of Freud's excursions into prehistory and history leave one with a strange impression. On the one hand, they are scarcely persuasive as history, on the other they may have some force as psychology. It is perhaps a pity that Freud was so obsessed with problems of historical origin. The objections, again briefly, to his supposed prehistory and history are these. First, totemism has been abandoned as a universal explanation of religious phenomena. (Incidentally, a new perspective on totemism has since been opened up by Claude Lévi-Strauss, in his *The Savage Mind*.[4]) Second, the father-figure is not always important in mythology; in many cultures the mother-goddess is more dominant—and in any case myths are richly peopled by deities and forces of various kinds, and to pick on the fatherly figures is highly selective, to say the least. Third, it is not after all probable that Moses was killed by his followers. Admittedly, some scholars are highly sceptical of the accounts of the Exodus, but this very scepticism would equally cut at the root of speculative reconstructions of the existing story.

But further, there is a methodological point of some importance emerging from a consideration of Freud's theories. The myths and rituals of religion are treated, perhaps justifiably, as like dreams, in the sense that their real meaning does not lie on their surface. Their real meaning has, in this case, to do with repressed desires, unconscious guilt-feelings, etc. But what criteria do we have for preferring one "secret" interpretation of myths over another? As we shall see, there are alternative accounts, such as those of Jung and Durkheim. One criterion might be: the interpretation works here and now in explaining the behavior and feelings of an individual who has a religious faith. It would look as though the most plausible aspect then of the Freudian account would be its contemporary psychological relevance, rather than its attempt to trace out alleged origins.

This, however, creates a difficulty in diagnosing the origin of past experience. It is well-known that psycho-analytic interpretations of past men is hazardous, for there is no possibility of digging down into the unconscious in a methodical way when the person is no longer available to the couch. Given Freudian methods, it is impossible that explanations of (say) Paul's conversion can amount to anything more than guesses. Still, if the methods work here and now, at least the results would be suggestive.

Probably they do so work in a number of cases of uncovering the roots of an individual's religion. It is plausible to think, as Freud maintained, that sometimes belief in God is an "illusion," in the rather special sense of the creation of a wish: men can thereby seek to restore the security of childhood by projecting a benevolent Father on the world (though a Father also with threatening characteristics, for the father frustrates the desires of the infant—but religion can supply mechanisms for propitiating the Father and averting the threat). But is it *always* an "illusion" in this sense? There are difficulties about universalising the judgment.

First, the shape of a religion is not determined by the individual. If then religion maintains over an historical period a relatively fixed structure, it is either because the latter is relatively independent of individual wishes; or because these wishes are rather stereotyped—everyone, for instance, goes through the situation of being brought up by parents and so has typical unconscious desires. The former solution means that psychoanalysis does not give a total explanation of religion; the latter solution itself creates the following and second difficulty. Some religions, as we have seen, do not pay all that much attention to Father-figures. Moreover, Theravada Buddhism treats the mythic with great irony. Are we to suppose that the early experiences of Sinhalese and Burmese differ radically from those of Western children? Even if we thought so, there still remains the problem that in the Indian tradition Buddhism coexisted over a long period under rather similar social conditions with Brahmanism and Shivaism, for instance—cults where a Supreme Being was quite important. Third, it is possible to find religious people who by ordinary standards of healthy realism, etc., have apparently got beyond religion as an "illusion." Thus, Roy S. Lee can write, not without plausibility, in his *Freud and Christianity:*

> It may be inevitable that almost everyone accepts and interprets the idea of God by way of wish-fulfilment. It is not necessary that the belief remain on this level. Indeed healthy religion will aim to take its adherents beyond it . . . The true "peace of God" does not confer protection. It gives strength and comes from accepting hardship and danger, and its distinguishing mark is that it shows a freely expressed love and service of other people.[5]

The second difficulty would perhaps show, if one were to remain committed to the rather "deflationary" account of religion contained in Freud's analysis, that theism, far from having its *origin* in unconscious wishes and fears, contributed powerfully to them. The destruction of theism would then become a goal for those who wish to make men more adult and healthy—but it would leave other faiths intact. This is virtually the line taken by Erich Fromm in his *Psychoanalysis and Religion,* where he distinguishes between authoritarian and humanistic religions—the former being incompatible with psychoanalysis as a method of therapy, the latter not.[6] Among the latter are numbered Buddhism, the religion of Lao-tse, that of Jesus himself, of Socrates, etc. As Walter Kaufmann has pointed out with some force (*Critique of Religion and Philosophy*), this division is riddled with difficulties and absurdities.[7] It is not true to the complexities of religious history.

What then can be said of the Freudian diagnosis? It is useless to neglect the great new perspectives which Freud opened up in the understanding of human behavior. The psychoanalytic and psychological investigation of religion has exciting possibilities. It cannot however be said that Freudian theory is much more than a first major attempt to come to grips with the problems. Since religion occurs in so many forms and has so many dimensions, it is not possible to divorce psychology from the comparative study of religion. The latter discipline was not well enough developed in Freud's day or well enough understood by him to provide the indispensable basis for theorising. What can perhaps be said positively is that Freud provides a partial explanation not of the origins of religion but of the reasons why certain forms of religion can more easily "catch on," and of the ways religious belief may sometimes be related to morality. It can also thereby help to explain why judgmental attitudes enter into a faith which yet preaches love, etc. Here we can employ an analogy.

Let us suppose that throughout the Steppes roughly the same climatic conditions prevail; yet there are marked differences of vegetation. In one area a certain type of grass has taken root, stopping soil erosion, and attracting various other kinds of plants; this in turn increases the moisture in the atmosphere, and one gets more rainfall, so that the grass and plants grow ever more luxuriantly (so much so that the grass itself is edged out from some districts). This model may be a plausible way of looking at Freudian explanations of religion: the climatic conditions are like the basic forms of psychological development; the grass is like some cultural-historical movement, such as Christianity; this in turn reinforces certain tendencies in the climate; and these help to reinforce Christianity and possibly to change it.

One final point about Freud's views must be made; for it is rather important philosophically. There is the suggestion that religion is likely to be an "illusion" because the reality of which it speaks (God) is not empirically observable. There is a prima facie unrealism about religious belief, and this gives credence to the idea that it is a projection. But this is to look at the phenomenon beginning from empiricist assumptions. This is not always a good way to start in the social sciences. It has been the basis of many misdescriptions in anthropology, for instance. Since other people do not conform to our ideas of rationality, it is easy to read into their behavior some form of "mystical," pre-logical mode of thinking. It is instructive in this matter to read the last chapter of Lévi-Strauss's *The Savage Mind*, where as a result of the examination of a wide variety of concrete instances he is enabled to conclude that "the savage mind is logical in the same sense and the same fashion as ours"—but the counters it uses are, of course, rather different.[8] Thus a sea-change might come over one's attitude to psychological phenomena if one begins from the belief in a universe one of whose constituents is the "other shore," the divine. In fact, this is where many people do start whose beliefs are being considered from a psychological perspective. It is then less easy to suppose that the non-empirical nature of their beliefs needs explaining. (Just as when I travel on the London underground dressed in white flannel trousers, my apparent eccentricity—to, say, an American observer—no longer appears as eccentricity when it is understood that I am on my way to play cricket, for which white flannels are normally *de rigueur*.)

Jung's attitude to religion is superficially more sympathetic than that of Freud, but more ambiguous nevertheless. Three features of his approach to religion are important. First, he rejected what he took to be reductionism in Freud's account—deriving religious beliefs from the operation of natural drives or instincts in interplay. He thus maintained that there is something called "spirit," the realm of religious experience. Since Jung believed that psychological problems were all (at least in his sense of the term) religious problems, then we must ascribe to the spiritual experiences which cure neuroses as much reality as the neuroses themselves: if religion is an illusion it must be a very real illusion. Thus Jung maintained an antireductionist position.

Second, Jung has perhaps a more cheerful view of the unconscious than Freud. It contains within it certain potentialities which if brought forth can lead to "individuation," the full realisation of one's selfhood. This second feature of Jung's thinking draws our attention to the point that value judgments necessarily enter into psychoanalysis and analytical psychology (Jung's term). For the theories are geared to practical, living, medical ends. The theories are designed to give people health or restore them to it. But what counts as mental health or its reverse is in part determined by what goals we think man ought to pursue, etc. So again a lot of difference is made by the starting-point one has. The production of Buddhist saints might, for instance, involve much tension in the initial stages and a withdrawal from ordinary adjustment to social living. If one thinks that the state of Buddhist sanctity is a noble and heroic goal, one can accept the tensions as "realistic." But if one prefers people well-adjusted to life in Westchester County, one would think of the tensions as "unrealistic" and damaging.

The third interesting feature of Jung's psychology is his twin doctrine of the collective unconscious and the archetypes. He was convinced from the dream and other material supplied by his patients that there are certain important recurring themes or symbols, the archetypes, which are somehow "collective." They exist in different cultures and different people, and cannot be explained in terms of the individual histories of those who bring them up. Characteristically, Jung is rather ambiguous about the status of the collective unconscious. Sometimes it seems like a single entity underlying the individual unconsciousness and consciousness; sometimes simply a set of inherited unconscious traits, standardised (so to say) as between individuals (like livers, which are inherited organs much the same in everyone). The former interpretation does not seem warranted by the facts: it is easier to think that people share archetypal images as part of their constitution. On the other hand, it needs some explaining to see how the latter sort of inheritance is, in detail, possible. It may be noted that a somewhat similar conception to Jung's was advanced by the pragmatist William James, for not dissimilar reasons—the discerning of recurrent patterns of religious experience, welling up, it seemed, from subconscious levels. (James, though, was more interested in experiences as such, Jung in myths and symbols, which have an indirectness about them—they express something obliquely: here again we meet the problem of the criteria of "secret" interpretation, of the rules for establishing the hidden meaning of the symbolic.)

The chief philosophical or methodological problem by Jung's use of the notion of archetypes is to do with the criteria of what indeed count as archetypes. This is a version of a general problem in the comparative study of religion: on what grounds are genuine likenesses established? The matter is more complicated when some symbol is also taken as expressing a hidden psychological meaning. Thus it may be that the circular mandala and its analogues express the need for (and the achievement of) an integral state of the self, the individuation at which Jungian psychology aims. But does anything round do so? In his later life, Jung diagnosed the flying saucer craze as a further instance; and indeed it is striking that so many should apparently want to believe in flying saucers. But how do we know the diagnosis is correct? After all, there are certainly some atmospheric phenomena which are like flying saucers in appearance: and much science fiction reading familiarises folk with the possibility of strangers from outer space. Putting the point more widely: the mythologies of the world are vast in quantity. Every so often we come across striking resemblances between the myths of one culture and those of another. But we have not exhausted all the possibilities of discerning recurring themes, for two reasons. First, nobody has taken a cool look at the whole mass of material; second, the meaning of a motif in a given myth needs to be seen organically in context—similarities otherwise unseen might thereby emerge, and by the same token some resemblances will be discovered to be just superficial. Until there is a fully developed and more scientific method of dealing with the whole problem, the question of recurring themes is largely to be answered intuitively and by guess-work. When the point of view from which resemblances are discerned (always important when intuition plays a big part) is itself speculative and ambiguous, it is necessary to be somewhat sceptical of talking about "results." This is a further confirmation that psychological theory of religion is still in its infancy.

A final word on Jung. His anti-reductionism does not, of course, amount to the claim that God exists because not derivable from prior psychological states, etc. Jung is notoriously ambiguous on this matter. He does not affirm the existence of God, but yet God can be "known." What he appears to mean is that the spiritual reality of which religious people speak is indeed a psychological reality, but there is no way of determining whether a transcendent reality corresponding to it exists. His remarks are made the more ambiguous by the use of the term "real" to mean "accepted as real"—religion must be "real" to a person to be spiritually healing: hence Jung's practice of sending people back to the religious institutions and teachings from which they started, those being "real" to them. Jung, then, while being anti-reductionist is not committed to faith in the existence of a supra-empirical reality. He takes the spiritual life as an important manifestation of human existence, rather. This is right in one way: the danger of reductionism is to render the phenomenon being reduced unintelligible (like trying to reduce music to arrangements of sounds, without seeing that music has its own form of manifestation, beyond the sounds, so to say). It could however have been hoped that Jung had been more precise both in his ontology and in his methods.

The third example of a theory of religion we shall consider is that of the sociologist Émile Durkheim. Here there is offered an explanation of religion in terms of social forces, rather than psychological ones. It shares with the other two theories we have contemplated the assumption that the apparent objects of religious practice (the gods, etc.) are not the real ones. There is a hidden object. This turns out to be society itself. As it happened, for accidental historical reasons, Durkheim was like Freud over-impressed by the importance of totemism. His anthropological studies had brought him into close contact with it; and reflecting on the way in which totems are coordinated to groups within society, he was inclined to stress very strongly the social function of religion. This prepared the way for a theory in which the social function became indeed the explanation of religion. The manner in which Durkheim worked this out, principally in *The Elementary Forms of the Religious Life*,[9] was subtle; but the main thesis was simple—that ritual cults, performed in relation to the sacred sphere, as distinguished from the profane sphere of everyday work, etc., were a symbolic acting out of the values of society, thus reinforcing the bonds of social relationships. The object, then, at which the cults were directed was, under a variety of symbolic forms, society itself. God is society writ large, and writ symbolic.

The importance of religion as the cement of society can lead, on the basis of Durkheim's thinking, to a sceptical and an optimistic evaluation of the role of religion. On the one hand, its truth evaporates if after all God is American society in disguise (some people think that the rather flourishing state of religion in the United States can be in a sense dismissed, for it is but disguised worship of the American ideal.); on the other hand, if Durkheim is correct, religion will not wither away, as (say) Marxism claims, with changing forms of society. New societies will need religions, perhaps new ones—like post-war Japan, with its efflorescence of new religions. (I call this an "optimistic" evaluation of the role of religion: but it could be pessimistic—it depends whether you approve of religion, etc.)

How can one judge this version of the "hidden meaning" of the objects of religious reverence? Religion seems to become something like saluting the flag, but unlike it also, because we perhaps know what we are doing in the latter case. The flag is already seen as a symbol representing the nation and so saluting it is explicitly a mode of expressing loyalty to the nation. (True, it sometimes turns out that the nation is idealised, but this ideal is firmly connected to the real nation). But in worshipping a god, a person is not explicitly directing his intentions towards his society, or at most only partially. This indeed is obvious from the very fact that a "hidden meaning" is being assigned to religious cults. But what does it mean to say that though I am worshipping Vishnu I am *really* reaffirming the values of society?

One thing it could mean is that I am only doing it because I have caught the custom from my culture; and my culture has the custom as a means of maintaining its stability. It might be that societies with unsuitable reinforcements of their institutional arrangements withered away, etc.: or there might be some other explanation of how functional religions become established. Then the claim that a society's gods are *really* itself simply amounts to the thesis that they have come to figure in society's imagination as a means of reinforcing social arrangements. One might say, Indians venerate the cow because (on this account) this veneration cements society; but it remains the cow that they venerate.

It is true that something can be unconsciously a symbol of something else, as in dreams, but one then has to spell out the elements of the symbolism and their connection with unconscious desires, previous elements of non-symbolic experience, etc. It is hard to see how this can be done in detail with religions, especially where they overlap different societies. (Thus the symbolism of Christianity is roughly the same in Spain and in Ireland, though the underlying societies differ.) One can, of course, modify Durkheim in the style of Kingsley Davis, in his *Human Society*,[10] and hold that sacred objects symbolise the unseen world, rather than society itself; then this unseen world gives a justification of the individual and group activities in society. But this modification is drastic: it means saying that religion has a function in society (say, in the terminology we have been using earlier, in terms of answers to limiting questions and in the subsumption of daily activities under ritual ones, such as worship), but that it has its own typical range of objects, even though the cult of these can be explained in terms of social function.

But it is not easy to know how one can show that the total explanation of religion is social, especially as what counts as social is an abstraction from the totality of human existence. (Is there not, for instance, room for individual psychological explanations of religious experiences, etc., which will then perhaps enter into the cultural stream through preaching, etc.?) It is not quite evident either why the objects of cults should symbolise the unseen world, rather than something else. (The United States flag is not taken as a symbol of the unseen God even if America be God's own country.) There are many chinks in such a theory which can serve to let in other partial explanations of religion. This is not to belittle the importance of Durkheim and functionalism in sociology. It is a strong affirmation of the social side of religion. Perhaps without the extremes of pure functionalism the social dimension and social roots of religious phenomena would have been neglected unduly. But it is not altogether persuasive.

The three theories we have considered so briefly testify to the beginnings of a fruitful age of enquiry into aspects of religion which have not been enough explored, partly because it is not until relatively recently that the social and psychological sciences have made a real impact on scientific, historical, and philosophical thinking. They also testify to the infant state of the enquiries, partly because the full richness of religious phenomena is only slowly becoming available through the comparative study of religion, anthropology, and the history of religions—themselves rather latter-day disciplines. And also, the three theories all present the problem posed by the attempt to say that the real object or meaning of religion is something other than that ascribed to it by the believer. This is not a matter of dispute about the truth of religion, though that comes into it (more clearly in Durkheim and Freud than in Jung); it is also importantly a question about meaning.

If the idea of the "real" meaning of something being something other than the meaning given by the person who holds to the myth or has the experience (the subject, let us call him) is to be worked out plausibly, the notion of the unconscious becomes highly important. Otherwise, the claim that the subject does not understand the real meaning of his experience, etc., is on a par with those theologies which from outside reinterpret another faith (as when the liberal Christian thinks of the Buddha as "really" having had an experience of God). Such a reinterpretation depends in part for its validity on the truth of the basis from which it starts. By analogy one might externally give an explanation of religion on the basis of an already accepted sociological or psychological theory. Then one fits one's presuppositions to the data supplied by entering sympathetically into the meaning of religion (or a religion). But surely religion itself is one of the important data with which to start. The imposition of a theory derived from elsewhere on religion may be unjustifiable, for if one started with religion together with the rest of the evidence, one might not hold the theory. Talk of the "real meaning" of religion may then be a sign that religion is being fitted to a Procrustean bed.

In short, much has to be done to make such theories viable. But they are a start, which is something. However, none of them give sufficient confidence for us to assert that the ultimate solutions to problems in the sociology and psychology of religion will be totally reductionist or deflationary.

For this reason, the truth of religious traditions remains an open question, and not one to be decided in advance by an adherence to philosophical scientism. But, as I said, it is not the main function of the philosophy of religion to argue for or against the truth of any particular faith, though it is its main function to bring out the criteria by which such decisions can be made. I hope that something of this has been achieved in these chapters.

Finally, I want to add a postscript about the questions which have not been tackled in this volume.

Notes

1. R. S. Peters, *The Concept of Motivation* (New York: Humanities), Chap. 1; and Ninian Smart, *Philosophers and Religious Truth*, Chap. 4.
2. Sigmund Freud, *Totem and Taboo* (New York: Norton, 1952).
3. Sigmund Freud, in Katherine Jones (ed.), *Moses and Monotheism* (New York: Random House, 1955).
4. Claude Lévi-Strauss, *The Savage Mind* (Chicago: University of Chicago Press, 1967).
5. Roy S. Lee, *Freud and Christianity*, p. 123.

6. Erich Fromm, *Psychoanalysis and Religion* (New York: Bantam Books, 1967).

7. Walter Kaufmann, *Critique of Religion and Philosophy* (Garden City: Doubleday–Anchor Books), pp. 236 ff.

8. Lévi-Strauss, *op. cit.*, p. 268.

9. Émile Durkheim, *The Elementary Forms of the Religious Life*, Joseph W. Swain (trans.), (New York: Collier).

10. Kingsley Davis, *Human Society* (New York: Macmillan), p. 529.

Postscript ࢱ

Since much philosophy of religion in the past has been conceived as a defence of, or attack on, theism at its vulnerable points (other than historical ones) much attention has been paid to the problems of evil, miracles, immortality, and the "proofs" of God's existence. The problem of free will has often figured in discussion too, because of its connection with the problem of evil and because of the (questionable) assumption that determinism is incompatible with religious faith. In recent times, attention has shifted very much to problems of verification and falsification, and attendant questions of the analysis of religious language. I have not attempted a full exposition or treatment of all these problems.

In regard to the analysis of religious language, I have said quite a lot, but more in the wider context of the analysis of the milieu in which the language occurs. Those who want a more "linguistic" treatment could consult my *Reasons and Faiths* and Donald Evans' *The Logic of Self-Involvement*, together with Frederick Ferré's *Language, Logic and God*, a useful guide to early postwar analytic philosophy of religion. I have discussed the major proofs of God's existence; but have only touched briefly on the problem of free will, but this topic belongs better in moral philosophy and philosophical psychology. If the problem has a real relevance to religion, it is in connection with particular religious views about God's grace, etc., and their relation to accounts of human choice. An example of the kinds of questions here can be found in John Oman's *Grace and Personality*.

The problem of evil has only touched on in the course of considering the argument about falsification and meaning. A good collection of papers on the general question can be found in Nelson Pike (ed.) *God and Evil*. About miracles, there are some interesting issues: here one can consult my *Philosophers and Religious Truth* (Chapter 1).

I have not discussed philosophical questions of personal survival, immortality, and rebirth, important as these are. There is not, as it happens, a big literature among philosophers of religion on these topics in recent years. A survey of some of the standard positions is found in C. J. Ducasse's *An Examination of the Belief in a Life after Death*; in Thomas McPherson's *The Philosophy of Religion* (Chapter 10), there is a clear account of the problems, in an up-to-date context.

There are other highways and byways we have not travelled; but philosophising is to do with a method of going about problems, as well as with a range of problems. The travel we have done may fit us to explore further, and perhaps may make us eager to go on. And as the Buddhist *Dhammapada* says:

"No mother, no father will do as much, nor any other of one's relatives: a well-directed mind will give us greater help . . ."

Index ❧

191